MAKE
A
MINT!

MAKE A MINT!

The Ultimate Guide to Buying and Selling Collectables

Jamie Breese

metro

Published by John Blake Publishing Ltd,
3 Bramber Court, 2 Bramber Road,
London W14 9PB, England

www.blake.co.uk

First published in paperback in 2007

ISBN-10: 978 1 84454 426 4

British Library Cataloguing-in-Publication Data:

A catalogue record for this book is available from the British Library.

Design by www.envydesign.co.uk

Printed and bound in England by Cromwell Press, Trowbridge, Wiltshire

1 3 5 7 9 10 8 6 4 2

© Copyright Jamie Breese 2007

Papers used by J   from wood grown
in sustainable fo   iental regulations

Every attem   de to contact the relevant copyright-holders, but some were
    unobtain   ontact us.
Captions mainly   some dealer prices e.g. telephones and TVs).
    These are a g   d packaging, are

The informatio   e and no liability
    can be acce   nnot guarantee
    financial ga   the use of the

FOREWORD

I WRITE THIS introduction to Jamie Breese's book as a fellow collectormaniac, having collected a great number of things over the past 60 years.

My collecting mania started after coming to England in 1935 when my father was made textile manager of a French woollen mill near Huddersfield. I arrived with just two words of English but was soon able to join many other lads at the exit to the local mill every 5 o'clock and ask, 'Got any fag cards mister?' Most boys collected cigarette cards and swapped them to build their collections. Cigarette cards and stamps seemed to be our main interest in the autumn and winter months; collecting and playing marbles was a spring and summer pastime.

Moving to Loughborough College and later working in a drawing office put a temporary end to collecting. We were then living in a large old house shared with the local veterinary surgeons. On investigating the surgery's cellar, I discovered a pile of old picture postcards – a treasure trove for the young collector! The collecting bug would

JAMIE BREESE

resurface years later after returning from the French army, getting married and joining the Mettoy Co. where the famous Corgi brand was initiated. I produced the first drawings of the very first model – the Ford Consul - followed by the Austin Cambridge and was made chief designer. I finished up responsible for every Corgi model in the range till the company's demise in 1983, and was involved in saloon and FI cars, army vehicles and many, many more designs. The scope was endless but limited by tooling cost, design and tooling capacity, but I always felt that each model must be topical, instructive and visibly acceptable. I definitely had one of the best jobs in the world and am so glad to see that all these years of production have created a fantastic following of collectors of Corgi Toys.

Why do we collect? Undoubtedly, nostalgia and memories of pleasant, youthful days figure highly. The attraction, as in all fields of collecting, is always to achieve a complete set. In the case of Corgi Toys it may just be a set of character merchandise or farming equipment. A complete set of the entire Corgi range would be very rare, as well as being extremely costly, though I know of one collector that has already spent over £250,000 on his collection! I haven't limited myself to collecting toys. At one stage my wife and I had over 33,000 postcards. In the past, collecting was done more by visiting junk shops and local auction houses. Today it is probably undertaken by attending car-boot sales and buying on eBay.

Jamie Breeses' *Make a Mint!* is the type of book that all collectors and would-be collectors need. It is full of very useful information on where to buy and where to sell. With his vast background experience he is able to pass on so much worthwhile and valuable information. And even if you do not make a mint yourself, the pure pleasure of collecting will be ample reward! My personal advice is to collect what you enjoy the most.

FOREWORD

At age 81 I have now disposed of nearly all my collections but still cannot resist a browse through eBay and can still be tempted…

Marcel

Marcel van Cleemput was the very first designer of the Corgi range in the mid-1950s. He is a passionate collector and author of *The Great Book of Corgi*.

PREFACE

BUYING AND SELLING collectables has never been more popular!
The huge rise in interest is down to TV, the rise of Internet auction sites,
our ever-increasing love of style and interior design, as well as a lack of
trust over some of the more traditional areas of investment.

Collecting is also a superb pastime and, for some, a way of life. When
I judged the entries for Corgi's 50th anniversary Ultimate Collector
competition in the summer of 2006, I was staggered to see the same
passion for the subject from every corner of the globe.

I have always advised people to buy with their heart first. After all,
they may have to live with it! Half the fun is either discovering that
something you have is of great value, or picking up such an item for a
song and then selling it on for a big profit. Hence the timeless popularity
of the BBC's *Antiques Roadshow*.

In addition, though the antiques trade as a whole has been
experiencing a relative lull, the individual has taken to the area of
antiques and collectables with enormous energy – partly by genning up
themselves, not only by studying their subject, but also by being prepared
to take the time to go out and buy and sell.

At the time of writing, I have been working with eBay.co.uk on their eBay Your Streets campaign and just completed writing their *Guide to Hidden Treasure*. It will be interesting to see how the rise and rise of the revolutionary online auction site affects the collecting world of the future.

Collectables, as opposed to traditional antiques, have shown the most growth. More recently, I have been predicting an explosion of interest in memorabilia, particularly that linked with celebrities. There are so many different areas to consider that I can only skim the surface, but – and here's the fun bit – it's completely up to you. Twentieth century objects are my main focus and most items referred to as a 'collectable' in this book come from this period. There's never been a better time to get stuck in and see what you might find. And you might even make a mint!

ACKNOWLEDGEMENTS

MY MOST HEARTFELT THANKS TO:

Patrick Stockhausen, Beju Shah, Martin Breese, Anthea Matthison, Nicky Evans, Martin Shervington and my other friends who have supported me while I have been hidden away writing my book.

A VERY SPECIAL THANKS TO:

Tina Weaver and all my colleagues and readers of the *Sunday Mirror* and more recently, *BBC Homes & Antiques Magazine*, *Women's Weekly*, the *Western Daily Press*, *Collect It* magazine and *Anitques and Collectables* for allowing me to share my passion for so many years.

Thanks to John Blake and my editor Clive Hebard.

The executives at ITV1, Channel 4, Five and the whole team at Hotbed for years of fun with *Everything Must Go!* Dawna Walter for inspiring me while we made *The Life Laundry*. Lastly, thank you to my friends at BBC2 for taking a punt on me back in 1998 and letting me loose on British TV.

Over the course of my years in the business, I have written many articles for some great magazines and I would specifically like to thank *Collect It* magazine, the *West Country Life*, *Western Daily Press*, *Northcliffe Press* and *Antiques and Collectables* magazine for kindly allowing me to reproduce and adapt some of them for use in the third part of my book.

CONTENTS

WHERE AND
HOW TO BUY

Happy Days! Helping a family Make A Mint! *in a classic episode of*
Everything Must Go! *for ITV1*© Jamie Breese

INTRODUCTION

THERE ARE SO many ways to buy collectables today! If you haven't already identified something that you have to sell, you might want to consider having some fun and going out and finding something cheap, marking it up and selling it – that's how you really make a mint.

In the following chapters of this part of the book, I am going to tell you about some of the best places to go to buy, the pros and cons of each route and also some insider tips on navigating them to enable you to be a success.

The best route – and I call these approaches to buying and selling routes – is actually something which most of us don't even consider. And this is one of my little secrets that I am going to share with you right now, for the first time… to whet your appetite.

In two words: for free!

I will give you one example from the off. Somebody I know bought a cheap copy of *Harry Potter and the Philosopher's Stone*. Just a hardback – not anything flash like a priceless first edition. Author J K Rowling was already well known, but not quite a superstar… and more crucially, she was still signing books fairly often. He simply looked on the web, found out where she was signing, paid his coach fair and queued. Within two hours he had a book that cost under a tenner, and was now worth £300-400. I also know a dealer who had a priceless first edition of the same book. By patiently queuing, he added around £2,000 to the value – with just one signature. It is not rocket science. Indeed, the whole market in philography (or autographs) and modern first editions has boomed in the last four to five years.

Before you read on, aside from your own possessions – take a moment out to think about all the possible routes you could follow to get hold of free collectables that can then be sold on for a profit. List them and you might be surprised to discover how many 'free' collectables are out there – from McDonalds Happy Meal Toys, to handbill 'flyers' promoting up-and-coming rock bands.

For everything else, just read on. I will lay out the basics and then give you the tips and tricks and true insights into how to buy some 'stock' ready for when you sell… to make a mint.

1

BUYING AT
CAR-BOOT FAIRS

IN THIS SECTION I want to share with you my best tips and tricks for
buying from my personal favourite which is car-boot fairs. The fact remains
that you need to have a keen eye and some basic knowledge if you are to
be able to sift through the clutter to snap up some collectable gems.

PROS OF BUYING AT CAR-BOOT FAIRS
- A real opportunity to find something incredibly valuable.
- I've said it many times, but they really do offer something to
  everyone. The myths about swathes of dodgy goods are largely just
  that – myths.
- I have never experienced any difficulties in my years of attending
  them. Car booters are hard working people having some fun and
  hoping to make a bit of cash or find something of use, be it a
  household item or better, an antique or collectable.
- There is one taking place near you – guaranteed.
- Low entrance fee – anywhere from free to a few pounds.
- The earlier you get there, the better the chance of bagging
  a bargain.

- Items are priced to sell. Towards the end of the day, you can pick up some pieces (if dealers and collectors have overlooked them) for a song.
- It's all small-scale stuff and, best of all, it allows people who are on low incomes to find cheap items that could normally cost them their weekly wage… and the odd collector or antique dealer to find a gem or two!

CONS OF BUYING AT CAR-BOOT FAIRS

- Weather can sometimes cancel a sale at the last minute.
- You'll have to rise mega early and queue to get real bargains.
- At many fairs, especially those in cities, you will be competing with clusters of extremely committed dealers and collectors. They know what they want and you will sometimes have to jostle for position and think really quickly when buying.
- Items should be taken as a/f (as found) and apart from querying whether something works or not, you don't have the same redress as you would have if you were buying from an antiques shop. Most collectables, strangely enough, aren't things that 'work' – you should be able to look at a teddy bear or examine a toy car. More often than not, you will be able to tell.

HOW TO FIND A CAR-BOOT SALE

- First up, you need to get a grip on the quality of fairs in your locale.
- Your local paper will often advertise where some of your nearest car-boot sales are.
- Some fairs run throughout the year, and these are often at covered locations.

> **JAMIE'S TOP TIP**
>
> Always keep your eyes peeled for those temporary roadside signs on gates to fields, outside schools and hospitals and on roundabouts in the middle of nowhere. These start to appear as the main season begins around Easter.

ON THE DAY

The entrance time for buyers is usually an hour or so later than for the sellers. That doesn't mean you can't get in the buyers queue early: the early bird really does catch the worm. The more stalls you get first pickings at, the more chance you have of making a mint.

DRESS CODE

- I would suggest bringing several layers: it can be bitterly cold in the early mornings, then, later, flaming hot during the summer days.
- Bring a bottle of water and a raincoat that stows in a small pouch.
- A bumbag is essential: make sure you bring plenty of change with you – the seller may not be able to change large notes. You are losing valuable hunting time if you are waiting for them while they ask other stallholders for change. You might even lose a purchase.

JAMIE'S TOP TIP

On the subject of clothing, here's a real insider tip: one thing I used to do, and it did seem to work, was to avoid wearing my Sunday best!

I would actually dress scruffily. Essentially it stands to reason: if you look, talk and even smell like you have lots of money, the sellers will see you coming… and you may end up paying more!

BE PREPARED AND MOVE QUICKLY

- The next thing is to pack several large laundry bags in a rucksack. These are standard issue for both buyers and sellers and can be incredibly useful if you come across a few rich seams to mine. They also have the benefit of hiding away nice bits and bobs which you have just picked up; to avoid showing your hand, as it were, to the other sellers.

- You run the risk of looking like an antiques dealer if you are flying around clutching great pieces of furniture and so forth. Again, you could pay a bit more if you look like a dealer – it's just a gut feeling I used to get.

- Based on my own experiences, I would urge you to move as swiftly as possible in those first 15 minutes. You need to literally fly around as many stalls as possible. Scan like a Terminator, and then move on. I would sometimes even run. A bicycle could be useful here.

- If you are the first in, you are usually competing with the professional antiques dealers or collectors who are highly experienced and need to find good stock quickly for their own businesses or passions.

- Keep mobile: avoid bringing pushchairs or kids if you are serious about finding nice pieces. If you are bringing your dog, then keep him on a lead at all times. Actually, just don't bring your dog.

JAMIE'S TOP TIP

I carry business cards with me wherever I go. On these cards, place your name, number and declare clearly that you BUY FOR CASH – and mention a few of the areas you are interested in e.g. first edition books, Royal Doulton figurines etc. Do not be afraid of giving these out to anybody! However, I would urge you to look for the car-boot sellers who have vans. These are more likely to be house clearance folk, traders or semi-professional booters who sweep up acres of stock each month. Beat everybody else – stack the odds in your favour – get closer to consistently finding items that will enable you to make a mint.

BUYING TECHNIQUE

- When it comes to actually buying, keep your poker face straight. If you see something that grabs your attention, keep calm, keep your hand on it (to keep others snapping it up) and ask the price.
- I can't overemphasise the importance of a detached demeanour. If you were to gaze longingly at a good original painting and started sobbing for joy, you are simply showing your hand and the asking price may strangely go up before it has even been quoted!
- If you like several items, quickly group them and negotiate a 'discount'.
- Sometimes the tables will be turned and you will be asked to make an offer for an item. Too high and you risk alerting them to the 'real' value. Too low and they might laugh at you and turn away. Try to avoid the question.

- Beware that £50 notes generally generate suspicion. Having cash in your hand, say a fiver, might just get you a £7.50 item merely because it's 'there'.
- Don't haggle with stallholders who are raising cash for charity.

WHAT TO BUY?

There have been several billion different objects created since the turn of the last century and I just don't have space here to list them all! Of course there are some basic rules that you should try and keep in mind when buying:

- Porcelain is always, always worth considerably less if it is damaged or showing signs of repair.
- Old toys are always hot, especially if relating to cult TV shows such as *The Avengers, The Muppets, Noddy, The Magic Roundabout* and *Doctor Who*. Movie toys are always going to find a home with the right collector: *Star Wars* (the first trilogy) is still HUGE, *Planet of the Apes, Blade Runner* (rare), *Star Trek* and the like.
- First edition books and other types of antiquarian titles have been steady areas of growth in the biz and many books are found first at the car-boot fairs around the country. Take a look at the special chapter in the third section and know how to spot a first edition novel and you could be in for a treat if you sift through enough boxes.
- Remember that, sadly, almost 99.9% of 78rpm records have little or no financial value. You see box after box at car boots. Don't waste time hoping to find one of the few rock and roll gems or early operatic recordings.

JAMIE'S TOP TIP

My best tip is to go to the third section of this book. Take a look at my personal favourite Top 20 collectables. This is designed to give you a good, solid overview of the types of collectables that are both popular and that make money.

Also, keep looking at my articles in the *Sunday Mirror* each week. You get a fresh, up-to-the-minute summary of all the latest developments, long before the guidebooks hit the shelves.

OTHER WAYS TO SPOT TRENDS

- Attend your local auction house and make a note of the prices lots are achieving. It's amazing how quickly you can get a snapshot of the current market for antiques and collectables by paying a visit to five or so sales.
- The auction catalogue should then start to form the beginnings of your own reference resource.
- Buying monthly magazines such as *Collect-it!* (which I write for) is another good way to get current info.
- The Web is incredibly useful, especially the mammoth worldwide selling tool that is ebay.co.uk. By watching the auctions again you get a handle on what sort of pieces to keep a look out for.
- For example, if you noticed a trend on eBay for early home computers and consoles a few years back, you could have cleaned up at the car boots and then re-sold on eBay or stockpiled for a year in the hope that prices would continue to rise.
- The list is endless. However, all these gems are worth considerably

more if they are in mint condition and boxed. If you have a choice, go for the best examples possible in the original packaging.

2

BUYING AT AUCTION

THE AUCTION WORLD is one that is full of colour. It is also one of the key routes that has been used for hundreds of years to make a mint. If you know your onions, you are likely to be able to navigate this route successfully and profitably.

In order to make a mint you need to know how to approach the auction room environment. It can be a touch intimidating for some, if they haven't experienced it before. I will lay out the key steps and offer my advice so you can go forward and take advantage of this wonderful trading post. It might be an idea if you also read through my other chapter about selling at auction, so you can understand both perspectives. That will only make you a wiser buyer and, of course, sooner, rather than later, you need to be selling on your 'stock' to capitalise on your efforts and make a mint.

Outside of the Internet business, there are two main types of auction: the specialist and the general sale.

Much of what follows will give you a handle on both.

The key difference is that the specialist sale is generally for the most experienced collector and dealer. It is usually full to the brim with items from one area only, say sporting goods, but then you do get the specialist sales with bells on at these events, e.g. rare cricket memorabilia that can sell for huge amounts. These type may only be held once or twice a year.

Assume the information and tips and tricks relate to the general sale – it is here that you will find all manner of tasty items.

PROS OF BUYING AT AN AUCTION

- The fact of the matter is that every day businesses fold, hundreds of individuals go bankrupt, families hold house clearances, repossessions occur and people just decide to sell their property.
- Visiting any auction provides an opportunity to look and learn (before starting to buy or collect), plus a real theatrical experience!
- Auctions are a buyers' market and deals are to be had for those willing to rise early and be persistent.
- The revolution taking place with online auctions and also online shopping has meant that, to a certain degree, there is less competition in the auction sale rooms. Folks are quite happy to be buying at home. This of course creates new opportunities for the canny local auction house buyer.
- There is little to rival the thrill of the real thing. Being in the auction room, seeing who you are bidding against, then winning the battle is a great buzz.
- You are able to take the purchased goods away there and then – unlike online auctions.
- By attending the view, you are able to truly establish a lot's condition for yourself.
- In the online auction game, you snipe and get sniped. Sniping is the art (often automated with software now), of outbidding other bidders at the very last second of an auction. Though standard

practice and part of the fabric, it is utterly frustrating and doesn't allow the determined buyer to react accordingly. In the real auction, you get a few moments to consider your position and raise the bid higher if you want to stay in.

- If you are shrewd, you can buy bargains in bulk at local auctions and then resell for a considerable profit online through sites such as eBay.
- Auction houses take a commission of between 10–15%, but a private dealer might mark-up by 200%+!

CONS OF BUYING AT AUCTION

- You are often 'competing' with seasoned, professional dealers and collectors who know the ropes and know the market, possibly far better than you.
- Items are sold as seen and there is little comeback if you find you have made a mistake.
- Sometimes cash or cheque is the only method of payment. Credit cards often carry a charge.
- You will have to factor in the buyer's premium and VAT on top when both planning and bidding. On large pieces of great value, this can be a lot of money.
- Though it is without doubt the exception to the rule, there have been a few instances of dishonesty and questionable behaviour from a handful of auction houses, which has been featured in the national press. In addition, the 'ring' of dealers conspiring to suppress the bidding is largely a thing of the past and laws have been bought in to protect buyers and sellers.

PREPARATION

Catalogues

This is of course one of the most familiar ingredients of the auction. They come in all shapes and sizes and are there to help you, the buyer, get a handle on what items are coming up for sale. These lots are listed in sale order and each one has its own number.

- Catalogues can be glossy affairs or, at smaller events, photocopies. Some houses charge around a pound, other larger or more specialist sales ask for £5–20.

- Estimates are provided with most lots. These are merely a loose guide – the value is only what two or more bidders are prepared to pay on the day, which is part of the fun. Estimates in general tend to favour the lower price to encourage bidders. If not printed they are sometimes shown in the salesroom.

- Catalogues make excellent reference material for your own use. I used to attend auctions, buy the catalogue and note down the prices that each lot achieved. This helped me to get a handle on the market in general.

- A catalogue is a sales brochure and won't always highlight bad points. Objects are bought 'as seen'. Always read the terms and conditions at the front to check guarantees. Many auctions have different terms. You will usually find a disclaimer that makes it clear that the auction house is not responsible for the origin, date, authenticity and condition. If you see the letters 'a/f', you can be sure that 'as found' probably suggests damage.

- Usually the terms will be inside the catalogue and will make clear the auctioneer's commission and the VAT information.

- If you are starting out, it might also be useful to note down the most you are prepared to pay for an item. This should factor in the various additional charges, like commission and VAT. By having a maximum price next to the lot, you lessen the chance of letting nerves get the better of you.

- The value of some auction catalogues can actually go up – especially if the sale was considered a classic. The photography and details often become part of an experts (or fans) toolbox for the future.
- The most valuable auction catalogue is linked to royalty. Limited editions of a Christie's catalogue of Princess Diana's dresses were sold for £1,250 in June 1997. They can now change hands for £25,000–35,000.

JAMIE'S TOP TIP

Did you see the money that changed hands at the auction of Princess Margaret's jewellery? Some lots went for ONE HUNDRED TIMES THE ESTIMATE! A pin bearing a single pearl was expected to command just £60. It sold for £6,000!

Estimates are a loose guide, not the final word.

The Viewing

This is your opportunity to get to grips with the items featured in the catalogue. It is known as a sale preview or just 'the view'. They sometimes take place over a period of a few days beforehand and, in many cases, on the day itself. It is important to confirm the viewing times by phone beforehand.

- In essence, each object's number tallies with the catalogue and you can make your way around the salesroom, closely inspecting the lots you are interested in.

- You can consult a staff member for advice about any item and request a closer inspection if your target lot is in a cupboard and locked away.
- One of the best things about auction views is the rummaging through the boxes of job lots. A job lot is a cluster of items, often a full box. These may not have been examined carefully by the valuers and precious items overlooked. Boxed job lots tend to be the reserve of the smaller auction rooms. There is always the chance of discovering a treasure – often referred to as a 'sleeper'. A great way to make a mint.
- My best advice here would be to thoroughly inspect and try to handle any item which you think is worthwhile – look at its condition and the possible cost of restoration. Remember, an item can be damaged between your inspection and the time the view ends.
- Occasionally the lot label can end up being accidentally placed over a blemish so do look, but always ask permission.

If you can't make it to the view, larger auctions will give condition reports on the phone.

JAMIE'S TOP TIP

Bear in my mind that another person may have also spotted your hidden gem and tucked it away at the bottom of the box! This isn't unheard of – and though unfair, is hardly theft. So you need to really check those job lots carefully.

THE SALE
Registration

You'll need to register as soon as you arrive. This is standard and gets you your paddle that you will later show to the auctioneer at the close of a successful bid. On the paddle will be your unique bidder number to identify you. You will need to provide some form of identification (so don't forget to bring some) and often a returnable deposit.

Buying Tips and Tricks

The sale begins and so does the fun! Sometimes, particularly in the smaller auction rooms, the speed of the sale is incredible – 100–150 lots per hour is the average. Ideally you will have nipped to the toilet first and found yourself a space at the back end of the salesroom so you can keep an eye on the other bidders. You know what you want, you have noted down the most you are prepared to pay and you are ready with your paddle.

How to Bid

There is no mystery to bidding. It is all straightforward and simply demands a cool and calm approach to get the best results. Here is the process, step by step:

1   The auctioneer calls out amounts in increments. Depending on the lot, these can be in pounds or sometimes in thousands of pounds. Bidding is over when the hammer (or gavel) hits the rostrum, usually preceded by the famous words 'going once, going twice...'

2   The auction-house porters (often wearing coloured aprons) will traditionally bring the lot in question to the front or at least stand near the piece and call 'Here, Sir', so all can see.

3   I would suggest trying to avoid being the first up to bid. Let things

play out. The auctioneer might even lower the starting bid to get things rolling.

4 Remember to keep eye contact with the auctioneer – raise your catalogue clearly to begin with – make yourself known to the auctioneer and just nod your head clearly for a yes if you are bidding against others, and shake your head if it has passed your limit and you are out.

5 Don't be afraid to call out, but if you are being ignored he may only be taking bids from two at a time. If one drops out he'll look around.

6 It's a myth that people accidentally indicate a bid by sneezing. An auctioneer will confirm the final bid by pointing and saying 'to my left' etc. If you really don't have the stomach, most auctions will ask a commission clerk to act for you for free!

Can't be There?

If you aren't able to be there for the sale, it is quite common to leave a 'commission bid' where you instruct the auctioneer to act on your behalf. They will go up to the amount you have written down previously. This absentee bidding often confuses the first timer as the auctioneer appears to be taking bids from an invisible bidder – he may say 'with me at…' to help clarify the fact he is working from the amounts set in the commission bids.

Again, most auction houses allow you to bid by phone. This is not as good as being present, but certainly better than leaving a commission bid. If you get stuck en route, this can be a lotsaver!

If you are a novice, you have nothing to fear, but always take account of commission and don't get carried away!

POST-SALE DETAILS

Payment

Payment should be made on the day of the sale in most cases. The rates vary but the buyers' premium (or the auctioneers-commission) will be added to the final 'hammer' price. It can be 10% or more. There is no VAT on the hammer price but it is payable on the commission.

JAMIE'S TOP TIP

The sale is over, but an item you like the look of hasn't sold... It is not uncommon to ask the auctioneer to flog it to you afterwards. You'll pay the reserve price if there was one.

Collecting

Once you have won the bid, the item is immediately your responsibility. It is good practice to 'clear' the item on the day. If you aren't able to, the cost of removing it is your responsibility. If you haven't cleared the item within seven days, and sometimes sooner, there are usually storage charges. In the worst case, an auctioneer has the right to resell the item if it remains.

Before you pick up an item check it – make sure it's in the same condition as when viewed. You might be able to clear the object while the sale is still in progress. If buying larger pieces such as furniture, check whether it is to be collected from the salesroom or the storage depot. Some auction houses have an arrangement with a transport firm. Check the details and consider getting a quote beforehand to better inform your bidding.

3

BUYING FROM
A SHOP

I THOUGHT I would offer some advice for you regarding antique dealers who have shops. I can make various suggestions based on experience. This book is called *Make a Mint!* but, in general, the truth is that unless you have expert knowledge which surpasses that of a specialist dealer, you are unlikely to take the item you have just bought from an antiques shop and sell it on immediately for a whacking great profit.

The high-street antiques shop is aimed at the general buying public, for people who want to find attractive pieces for gifts or for their own personal enjoyment. They are looking for the guarantee of quality and comeback that a shop can offer. The simple reason is that dealers in a shop are hard-working individuals who have to make profit to cover their overheads, which can be substantial.

Traditionally, the high-street price will be noticeably higher than if you were to locate the item yourself at a local auction house, charity shop or car-boot fair. But there are many exceptions to the rule:
• Buying from dealers at antiques fairs is one of the exceptions (see Chapter 4). This is a source for many other dealers' stock and bargains can be found aplenty.

- If you are prepared to sit back and allow some years to pass, then there is a strong chance your investment in an item or portfolio of items will appreciate in value. Sometimes, it can be just a couple of years.
- If you are buying from a dealer in another part of the world and then selling in your home country, or vice versa. It is well known that Americans and Japanese will pay more for genuine European antiques and collectables in their home country than they would if they shopped around in, say, England.
- There can be flexibility. If a dealer has had an item in stock for some time, they might be prepared to get shot of it at a knockdown price for cash.

THE PROS OF BUYING FROM A SHOP

- Some shops are cluttered and contain corners stacked with goodies from which bargains can still be found.
- Some dealers will want to develop a relationship that will last. For example, I have one with Adrian Harrington Rare Books in London where I will turn to source the finest possible rare books. Unlike many auctions and certainly car boot fairs and charity shops, you will get an opportunity to discuss the stock, your requirements and other matters in some depth.
- If you develop that relationship, the dealer will often act as a superb expert and far-reaching set of 'extra eyes' for you. If you know that you can sell certain items for a profit elsewhere, a dealer will often learn your 'shopping list' and will call you if he has an item of interest or can get something for you. You set the price there and then and know you will get first dibs. Dealers often deal with each other, not just with collectors. If you are buying strictly to sell, then you need to develop the dealer mindset and become a dealer yourself.

- If you are looking for a certain collectable – whether for yourself or because you know you can sell it on elsewhere for profit, then you will save yourself a lot of time trawling around auctions and car-boot sales.
- You are buying from a source that provides some comeback for you and can recourse to action if you feel you are mistreated.
- Many reputable dealers are members of a trade body e.g. the British Antique Dealers' Association (BADA) that vets its members and demands certain standards through the code of practice. The dealer might also be a member of a specialist association, so Harringtons, for example, is a member of the Antiquarian Booksellers Association (ABA).
- If you purchase an item through a BADA member and you find they have made a mistake in the description, invariably this will entitle you to a full refund. If it can't be settled this way, BADA offer a free arbitration service.
- Many antique shops will offer a free local delivery service.

THE CONS OF BUYING FROM A SHOP

- Antique shops generally deal with the buying public. Making a mint is less easy unless you have in-depth knowledge on certain areas or indeed, are a fellow dealer.
- Dealers need to mark up their stock to cover their overheads and to make a profit. They will not usually buy at 'book' price (or the value of an item as listed in a current price guide).
- If you buy with a card, remember that credit card companies take a cut of the dealer's price, which is reflected on their price tag.
- If you want to buy and then quickly re-sell for profit, your margin will be slight unless you have a network of customers yourself, who you also know will pay top whack for the right piece.

PAPERWORK AND PAYMENT

When you buy from a shop make sure you get the paperwork. There are clearly benefits to this. You need to ensure you get all the pertinent details down on the invoice – this will help a re-sell in the future, help you with insurance, keep the tax man happy and allow you to dispute claims clearly if for some reason you find that your item is not authentic or of the era you were told, and so forth.

Deposits may be requested if you ask for the item to be held for you while you check with a partner (or another customer of yours if you are selling on). I found often that folks would come by, say they were going to purchase an item of my stock or go and get the chequebook, and then you'd never see them again.

My best advice when buying an item from a dealer is just to be open – tell them honestly what you are planning and see if there is flexibility in both price and any other terms. Dealers in general don't stand behind a stall at a car-boot fair. They are professionals and need to be treated as such. Especially when it comes to haggling! For sure, if you don't ask, you don't get; but don't expect to go in with the same tactics I have raised in the buying at a car-boot fair section.

I have heard of some regular punters (i.e. you and me), pretending to be trade. Not only is it unethical but you can also lose your legal protection as a regular consumer. It's really not worth the risk.

Bargaining is more likely to work in your favour if you are paying with cash and say you are going to take the piece away with you that day. Remember that you are paying for expertise and a service and there may be little or no flexibility on the price tag in many cases.

JAMIE'S TOP TIP

A relationship with a dealer of any type can be worth its weight in gold. You should collect their business cards and if you buy from them, tell them to stay in touch. Ask if they have any similar stock and get them to call if they see something you'd possibly like. With a dealer, it is about relationships if you plan to be making a mint in the long term.

EXPORTING

Just a quick note for you if you are planning to export your finds. This book is focused on collectables – mostly items made in the last one hundred years or so. However, the British government has put thresholds in place for items over 50 years old and around £65,000 or more. Below the threshold means you don't require a licence, but there are clear exceptions to this that you need to know. You'll need to check this with the dealer or with the Export Licensing Unit. It is not all that complicated, but you must get the facts and know them before you decide to make a purchase of size.

With certain items – particularly antique firearms and certain objects made from protected species – you will need to obtain a licence to export. Keep these details to hand, as you will need to make contact if you have any questions that a dealer can't help with. Sometimes a dealer can manage the paperwork for you – another benefit.

For more information, contact The Department for Culture, Media and Sport, Export Licensing Unit, 2-4 Cockspur Street, London SW1Y 5DH, 020 7211 6164.

4

BUYING AT
ANTIQUES FAIRS

YOU MAY HAVE seen the signs for them, or perhaps even taken a look around one in your spare time. This book is about collectables and you will find plenty of them at antiques fairs.

There are lots of vetted fairs out there that take place all over the country, sometimes only once a year. These are where dealers' wares are adhering to a dateline, often a specific area and level of authenticity. They are a bit like an antiques shop on the move and are a great place to meet experts and often find superb pieces.

I am going to focus on the more general, often outdoor fair, which features all manner of items and does not fall into a strictly vetted type of event. The general antiques fair is a staple part of the business and is where a good deal of both regular punters (the buying public) and the trade (other dealers) get to buy fresh and often good-value collectables, outdoors or indoors.

Being without a car when I was a nipper, I didn't explore them enough and lost out on the huge potential awaiting each visitor among the thousands of stalls. I have several friends today who still pay the key UK fairs regular visits. One has a shop in London and frequently finds great items to add to his stock or sell directly to his contacts around the world.

THE PROS OF BUYING AT ANTIQUES FAIRS

- A huge array of antiques and collectables in one place.
- A chance to bag a real bargain.
- It's not a car boot – each stall will be laden with items of interest, mixed with plenty of pieces of substantial quality.
- Fast-moving and can take home that day.
- Buyers get to see the items in person and make a decision on the spot.

THE CONS OF BUYING AT ANTIQUES FAIRS

- If you want to be first in, you need to be prepared to queue for some time at larger events.
- You need to travel and possibly stay overnight. Fairs are spread out around the country. If you want to buy bigger collectables, an estate car or van is often required.
- You are often among thousands of other eager buyers including professional dealers and experienced collectors.
- You need to be quick on your feet and able to make firm decisions at the top of the day to get to and secure the best bargains.
- Cash is king – you need to take a lot of it with you. Not ideal but standard in the trade.
- Some desirable items might be put aside for buyers with whom the stallholders have an existing good relationship.
- You usually have to take away on the day, though some dealers will make alternative arrangements for large or bigger ticket items.

Jamie's Tips and Tricks

Quite a lot of the advice I offered in the chapter about buying from shop-based dealers also applies here.

1 You should phone the organisers the day before to check the event is still on. Basic stuff I know, but it can save a lot of heartache.

2 As with any shopping trip, you need to have a clear idea about what you are focusing in on. If you have gained knowledge about Corgi toys and have decided to buy good examples at bargain prices to sell on eBay, then stick to the plan – do not go looking for autographs or early gramophones. If you know what you are looking for, you'll be amazed at how one is able to filter out everything else and nine times out of ten, your quarry will present itself to you.

3 As with car-boot fairs, the early bird often catches the worm. Though you are not a dealer, you need to develop the same mindset to make a mint!

4 A combination of politeness and brevity is a really good approach to adopt, especially if you decide not to buy something on display after discussing it. These are busy people who can spot time wasters a mile off.

5 Some enthusiastic buyers will make their way around outdoor fairs on pushbikes or even mopeds! I sometimes think you get to miss out on the close inspection that the feet allow!

JAMIE'S TOP TIP

You will find that many stallholders will keep items aside once they have been paid for in full. Then, at the close of play, you can go back and collect your new finds. This helps keep you mobile.

MANNERS COUNT

Only pick up an item if you have asked and are genuinely interested – that's good practice. For sure, you must check for damage especially if the price label says 'a/f' (as found).

I used to be amazed at how many punters would pass my stall and pick up an old item and tell me, 'I've got one of these in my attic.' This is so frequent that I know of a dealer who called his company I've Got One of Those in My Attic!

MONEY MATTERS

As suggested, cash is the preferred payment at antiques fairs. Some organisers can take cards but the charges that dealers incur make it less attractive for them, plus in some cases they need to wait quite a time to receive payment.

My advice would be to ask if the stallholder takes cheques or cards upfront, before talking turkey. That way they will know the deal and will avoid the surprise once you've agreed the price.

Most pieces will be priced up. If not, the label has probably fallen off. Politely ask. If you are trade, which you are most likely not, you ask for the 'trade' on it. There are almost set rules to trade haggling. If you're not, you can see if there is any leeway, or just pay the price as displayed.

A no means a no from a dealer. Don't push it, but don't be afraid to ask to see if there is a little flexibility at the top, especially on items of some value and you've got cash. Never offer silly money — and that includes half-price offers! That is bordering on insulting.

Make sure you get a receipt. This is for tax, your own comeback and insurance.

Lastly, when I have bought from fairs, I have taken my own bags and some bubble wrap to ensure any gems get home in one piece and I recommend you do the same. Better safe than sorry!

5

BUYING AT A HOUSE SALE

OVER THE YEARS, I have organised dozens and dozens of house sales in my capacity as presenter of ITV1's *Everything Must Go!* Buying from a house sale is quite straightforward and indeed, a few of the tips and tricks you learnt in Chapter 1 about buying from a car-boot fairs can be applied here.

THE PROS OF BUYING FROM A HOUSE SALE

- Because of the potluck nature of the game, you may well be able to spot something of value and take a punt – if you know your onions.
- You are far less likely to be competing against dealers, collectors or indeed 'Make a Minters'! House sales are advertised locally and sometimes only by word of mouth, so you have a fine chance of bagging a bargain.
- The overall number of punters might be low, especially if it has not been promoted well (as I suggest in the chapter dedicated to selling through a house sale).
- Everything Must Go! It's true, but in my experience, most of the leftovers get taken away to the charity shop or worse, thrown away.

THE CONS OF BUYING FROM A HOUSE SALE

- In general, buying from a house sale is not one of the key ways you are going to make a mint.
- They don't occur all that often in the UK.
- There are generally a limited amount of items to buy – certainly not the stall-after-stall of pickings that a car boot proffers.

BASICS

- My best advice would be to turn up early to get in the queue.
- Bring a couple of laundry bags to take away any finds.
- Bring cash only!
- Look for a job-lot deal that you can take away at the end for a snip and then re-sell at a car boot or online. While these won't be collectables, you can still make a profit on household goods – and you're not afraid of earning that extra cash when an opportunity presents itself, are you?!

JAMIE'S TOP TIP

If you are able to, see what's left at the end of the day, make an offer – then fill up the car boot and take it off the next day to the local car-boot fair. You can almost guarantee you will make a tidy profit.

6

BUYING USING EBAY

THIS CHAPTER IS written to give you the confidence to go out there and get started as soon as possible. eBay is clearly one of the best routes to making a mint and you are missing out if you are not scouring this amazing site looking for bargains which you can either keep, add to a collection or re-sell for a profit.

eBay is just like a massive electronic flea market, house sale or car-boot fair. How to use eBay is a vast subject and I can't cover it completely in this chapter. What I can do is give you the incentive to get in there, get registered and get trading! Then I will provide you with the best step-by-step tips and tricks and some really solid advice from my experience. I have helped all sorts of people make a mint from eBay. Indeed, I published four issues of my column in the *Sunday Mirror* with some great information for millions of readers to enjoy and then use to make a mint themselves.

---

eBay is Huge!

- eBay.co.uk hit the 15 million users milestone in April 2006 and continues to go from strength to strength. The site has proven to be one of the most revolutionary uses of the Internet and at any given time, there are approximately 60 million listings on eBay worldwide.
- It is also the UK's most-visited eCommerce site. Online trading can be a great source of secondary income, and for some, a huge primary business.
- eBay was founded in 1995 and offers registered users a chance to sell or buy virtually anything. You can either bid for items or take advantage of a feature called 'Buy It Now' for a fixed price. Once you have ten transactions under your belt, you get a yellow star and the option of using the Selling Manager tool that streamlines your work.
- Trust is a big factor and gaining negative feedback is a something that can ruin users' reputations, so there is little monkey business. eBay now own PayPal too, which is one of the best ways to make payments.

RECORD BUYS

Some strange pieces have come up in the past including dinosaur skeletons and a wedding dress modelled by an ex husband! One of the most remarkable buys I have heard of was the sale of 'Nothing – not even a pound coin'. This made an amazing £51!

The most expensive item sold on eBay to date is a private business jet for $4.9M. A handbag once owned by Margaret Thatcher once sold for £103,000; Joanna Lumley's Ferrari was sold for £35,000; from cornflakes (£1.20) to the original Hollywood sign (£450,400) there really is something for everyone! eBay should be your first stop when researching collectables online.

THE PROS OF BUYING FROM EBAY

- A worldwide shop window and a genuine revolution in trading.
- Millions of items available for purchase at any given time.
- Straightforward to use.
- An auction in your living room – you don't have to travel anywhere!
- The chance to pick up truly amazing bargains.
- You can buy cheap at a local Sunday car boot, have it on eBay by lunchtime, and sold for a profit – sometimes VAST – by suppertime.
- The Buy It Now feature on some items removes the waiting game and the chances of losing the item to somebody else in a bidding frenzy.
- In the UK there is a buyer and seller protection programme on certain listings.
- The more you use it, the sharper your skills.
- The possibility of conducting ALL your buying and selling via this route.
- It is not just antiques and collectables – you can buy virtually anything.
- It is a viable online price indicator.

THE CONS OF BUYING FROM EBAY

- Bad feedback as a buyer can permanently damage your chances of future trading (buying *and* selling).
- Not all sellers accept all types of payment.
- There are usually postage charges involved, sometimes handing charges too.

- If you have no computer, or no computer skills, you are not going to be able to participate easily. You can always rectify this of course!
- You don't usually get the opportunity to inspect the goods in person, as in a real auction room.
- There is no real, independent middle man as with an auction house.
- The virtual reality of this type of buying doesn't appeal to everyone. You can spend hours in front of your computer before you find what you want.
- Just remember that with any kind of buying, there are scammers out there. You may have heard of a few stories, especially in the late 1990s, where people were ripped off, bought items only to receive nothing, or received items that didn't match the description. eBay now offers more help with these kind of situations and they remain the exception rather than the norm.
- eBay performs best if you have a broadband connection to the Internet and not so well if you still have dial-up.

GETTING STARTED

The good news is that you don't have to register to browse this wonderful site. You simply click on to www.ebay.co.uk and then follow the advice below to perform your searches.

If you want to buy or sell, you need to register and for this you will need a credit card. You will also need to decide on a user name and password. Avoid using the same for both! Let's say you have registered and taken the simple steps to opening your own eBay account.

Let's also say you collect Corgi toys. You are on the look out for the famous silver Aston Martin DB5 James Bond car. There are a few ways to find one on eBay – in the listings. You can effortlessly search by either:

The 'Title' (and within that you can do the basic or advanced routes.)
The 'Bidder'.
The 'Seller'.
Using eBay Shops.

What's really handy is that you are able to actually save your favourite searches in the Favourite Searches part of My eBay. It saves time and makes things nice and organised. Also, as the buyer, you can search for your Corgi Aston Martin in either the All Categories page or a specific category. When starting out, it is probably best to use the All Category option as it is really straightforward and immediately comes up with a whole host of items. Try to avoid using 'noisy words' such as 'and', 'the' or 'or'! Don't be concerned about capitals and lower case – it doesn't alter things in search terms.

In this case you would be best to enter: 'Corgi Aston Martin DB5'. Also, I would advise you to 'search within item and description' to give you a better chance. If you get too much to wade through, you can then start to refine your search. If you are new to eBay, confine yourself to searching within the UK. Indeed, few sellers are prepared to ship worldwide. Save this for later when you have some neat items to sell.

You will then be presented with Buy It Now options and the more familiar auction options – where you need to wait until the sale ends (most items are sold in a 7 day scenario).

RESEARCH

Before you bid on any item, especially if you are just starting off, it is important to research the item you are interested in. Fortunately, you are in a really great position as you have one of the best researcher's tools right in front of you – the computer and Internet. Better still, eBay itself is the best tool of all!

You can go back and search auctions that have finished and get a grip on the prices things are fetching by looking at these results. Make sure you perform the straightforward completed listings type of search. In our example, you will quickly know how much a mint and boxed Corgi Aston Martin DB5 Bond car is currently making – and you are less likely to pay over the odds as a result! You should also check a price guide if you have one – just to get a balanced opinion. Google is a good search engine to sift around and see what a toy dealer or other auction has sold one for. Remember to check the dates of the sale too, as prices can change very quickly, say if a new Bond movie is coming out.

POSTAGE

Make sure you check what the postage costs are likely to be. These are usually passed on to the buyer and can be substantial, so be absolutely sure you factor the costs into your eventual bidding strategy or you can really lose out. With our Corgi car, the UK postage of recorded delivery isn't going to be too much. If you buy the real thing (and it happens), we are talking a different story I think! There is usually an option for insuring your item. Check with the seller for details.

KNOW HOW TO ASSESS TO AN ITEM

Make sure you can see a photograph of the item – most sellers will provide pictures of anything of value or of note. You can always ask for one if you want to be sure. If needs be, contact the seller before you start bidding on an item: click on the 'ask seller a question' box to do this. It's all in the main listing window and very easy to get to. Ask standard questions such as 'Is it complete?', 'Does it work?', 'Is it still boxed?' and 'Are their any special postage costs involved?' These questions really should be addressed in the item's description on the site.

You can also ask for further photos. If the seller has described 'some damage' ask for a close-up picture to be sent to you. You should also be certain that the item you are interested in is legal and permitted for sale by eBay. Check eBay's policies on the site.

CHECK THE SELLER'S FEEDBACK

Here's a great thing about eBay. You get to see, with a click of a button, what sort of person you might be about to do business with. For a long time there has been a buyer and seller feedback system where people who have traded with each other can leave comments about their experience. It is an essential part of the entire eBay world and should be your first port of call.

Indeed, it is really important that the feedback rating is displayed alongside each item up for sale so that you can work things out for yourself at a glance. When you have ten positive feedbacks deposited, you receive a gold star, after one hundred it turns blue, 500 makes it purple and 1,000 gives you the mighty red. These stars are very important to buyers and sellers in equal measure. Be certain to check the last few transactions either way.

JAMIE'S TOP TIP

It is worth bearing in mind that a seller might have a great feedback score, even up to 100%, but that may have been as a buyer. Perhaps they have never sold before so in one sense you could be dealing with a newcomer who hasn't proven anything. Be mindful of this with big-ticket items and ask questions if needs be.

READY...

You have found your silver Corgi Bond car. It is for sale in the conventional auction manner (as opposed to the Buy It Now or the more flexible Best Offer sale). You are ready to bid! It is very straightforward. You click on the item and you will be taken to the auction item page. This page contains all the information you need and it's nicely laid out. You will see, from top to bottom, key details including:

- The category of the item – in my experience you will most likely find this gem in: Toys & Games > Diecast & Vehicles > Corgi > Novelty, Film & TV.
- The title of the item and its own number.
- A photograph of the car – usually with an option to zoom in.
- The current bid. If nobody has bid, then the amount is the Starting Bid in eBay terminology.
- You might also see the words Reserve Not Met or Reserve Met. This means that the seller, as in a conventional auction, has set themselves a minimum amount that they will accept. This reserve, again as tradition dictates, is also hidden and is not always set by the seller.
- Alongside the current bid amount, you will find that all-important Place Bid button. More on that shortly…
- Then, just to the right, you will see the Meet The Seller area. Lots of info is displayed in a small space and it refers to the feedback matters we discussed earlier.
- Underneath the Place Bid button you will find information about the auction end time, postage details, the item location, the bid history (telling you how many bids have been made so far) and lastly, the current highest bidder. This obviously changes if you enter a higher amount.

- Pay special attention to the Bid History as it gives you an indication of how desirable that item is – and how many other folks are going to be trying to wrestle it away from you as the time draws closer and closer to the end of sale.
- The incredibly useful Watch This Item button is worth its weight in gold. You click and the item is added to the My eBay area of the site. This is your own little space to keep track of what you are bidding or selling. You don't even need to be registered – there is a guest area. Superb for those just dipping their feet in, looking at prices and not wanting to dive in just yet.

So there is a degree of transparency here – you can see who is bidding and they can see you. Often, if you are interested in the same sort of collectable, you will see these sellers' user IDs time and time again!

ITEM DESCRIPTION

One of the key boxes is underneath all of the above – the Description. Here is as little or as much as the seller wants to tell you about the item. There will often be a few more pictures and other key comments. You might find the exact postage amount mentioned here too. Ask yourself what is mentioned and also, what isn't mentioned. It's standard sales technique, trust me, to focus on and list only the positives. Save yourself a lot of potential heartache and really scrutinize this all-important area of the page.

PAYMENT METHODS

Next, you need to see how the seller wants to be paid. The most popular methods are a personal cheque and PayPal. PayPal is now owned by eBay, so there is continuity here. I like PayPal and there is no charge for the buyer. It also operates around the world in quite a few countries – certainly most of Europe and the USA. PayPal also keeps your card and account details strictly confidential. There is also a nifty benefit too: quite a few purchases can qualify the buyer for the Buyer Protection Programme. There are lots of other options from banker's drafts to credit cards. There are pros and cons to most options. Just don't send cash!

PROXY BIDDING

eBay uses a system which isn't dissimilar in many ways to the experience of a real auction-room sale. By entering your maximum bid amount, clever eBay will automatically keep bidding up to that amount, if necessary, on your behalf... and better still, you don't even have to be there watching it. It is called bidding by proxy.

We will look at placing a bid next... but, if the Aston Martin you've set your heart on is currently at £100, and you have entered £150 as your maximum bid, then your proxy bidder, acting on your behalf, will automatically raise your bid incrementally in reaction to other peoples' bids, up to your £150 maximum.

The other users will not know if you are sitting there watching and entering in little amounts to keep the ball in your court, or whether you are not around and have left it to your proxy. It is a bit like the absentee bidding mentioned in the auction chapters, where the auctioneer bids on your behalf, in your absence, up to that fixed amount you set before the sale – the auctioneer knows it, nobody else.

Sure, others will probably still be bidding away on your Corgi car – they may well pass your maximum bid, so you will have been outbid. If you're there, in the haze of it, and the price is within your pre-established maximum (the promise you made to yourself at the start), then enter another amount, possibly a small amount, just to try and pip the other person. Then again, perhaps you have set a reasonably high maximum bid in the first place, gone off to walk the dog and left it with your proxy bidder (not a real person I should add). You may just manage to fend off the competition as the proxy reacts and ups the ante on your behalf. The other bidders will know really quickly if they are still in as they are told by email or can see it for themselves that they have been outbid.

There is a whole art to the final stages of bidding, sniping and similar, and software has even been developed to do this sort of stuff.

PLACING THE BID

So, to backtrack slightly here, you have found your Corgi Aston Martin DB5 car and have left it to the last hour or so — when most of the bidding activity often takes place — and you are set.

I would take a leaf out of the traditional auction route book: decide beforehand how much you are willing to pay and stick to it rigidly. This is by far the best strategy for the buyer at any level. Keep a calm head and don't get carried away. Knowing your limits is the only way to consistently avoid heartache and get yourself into a situation later, where you end up paying over the odds or worse, trying to wriggle out of it, which will lead to bad things!

1 Click on either of the two Place Bid buttons. One is at the top of the auctions item page; the other is at the very bottom.

2 You will be taken to a new page where you will be asked to place a bid. If the Buy It Now option is available, you will also find the button here.

3 You will need to be logged in to place your bid. Look at the current amount and decide on your maximum bid (at this stage). It clearly needs to be higher than the current high bid.

4 Next up – you will be taken to the Review Bid page. This is effectively your last chance saloon! Look carefully at the amount you entered. Did you miss the vital decimal point or include an extra zero? Look carefully, then click on the Submit button.

5 Please remember that your bid is a binding contract – you absolutely have to stand by it as retracting a bid can prove rather tricky and if late or without a really good reason, you are heading towards the bad feedback page faster than you can imagine.

6 eBay will send you an email to confirm this but not always as quickly as you would like. Why not keep track of the situation in your My eBay pages? It is all crystal clear there with colour-coding for the current status – green for in, red for out.

7 Hopefully, you will be the current High Bidder and you will see your user name on the actual auction item page. If this is a first-time bid, then well done. You've just entered an exciting new world and I hope you will be using this technology to make a mint, and quickly.

8 Let's say the End Time of the sale is coming up. A clock will be ticking down – maybe you have kept yourself in by being there and raising your maximum bid to your maximum amount – and your competition bows out. You have won the item fair and square and will be sent an email pretty promptly. Sometimes the seller, if really keen, will beat eBay to it with an email informing you and politely relaying all the key info you need to complete the transaction.

By the way, neither the buyer nor the seller has any say over the increments: they are set by eBay automatically using clever science stuff! This bid increment is the amount by which a bid is raised and can be by 25 pence, £1, or many pounds at a time! It depends on many factors.

You will need to make sure your bids are within the acceptable increments. Proxy bidding automatically covers this.

JAMIE'S TOP TIP

There are several other ways to buy:

- Buy It Now. Perhaps the listing you are fired-up about has the Buy It Now (BIN) option displayed? If it does, then do look at it seriously – if you think you can make a mint on it, then consider going for it there and then and thereby avoiding the bun-fight that can be a standard auction.

- Consider Best Offer. If this feature is displayed, then you can present a price that you hope will be agreeable to the seller. It's a more flexible version of the Buy It Now feature, offering a way to get the item you want right away. In some categories, you and the seller can counteroffer each other until you come to a price you both like.

YOU'VE WON! NOW ACT QUICKLY

This is my best advice. You will receive an End of Auction message from eBay reminding you if you were not online during the final stages. Your My eBay page will also have details telling you what to do next.

eBay asks for the two parties to get in touch with each other within three working days of the close of the auction. Think of it like a traditional auction sale – you don't want to be stuck in the salesroom waiting around or leaving the goods to be collected for long. Just follow the instructions for payment – always be polite and make sure you don't delay payment.

Get things right your end and you will:

- Establish the best habit from day one.
- Keep your feedback nice and clean.
- Not leave things open to chance (e.g. being called away unexpectedly).

Using PayPal is usually just a click and it is done. Sending a cheque obviously requires time but has the benefit of also leaving a clear paper trail. Your seller will remind you how much the total is with postage. Either way, keep print-outs of the actual final auction page. If paying by cheque or postal order, be sure to send a copy of the print-out with payment so the seller is clear what is what. It is just good form and helps you to keep track in the long run. You will also have a record by email that can be useful if you ever need to dispute matters down the line.

If you do not hear from the seller and things are not looking so great, you can contact the seller by using the Find Contact Information option. eBay will not only send an email to you and the seller, but will provide you with the contact info including a telephone number.

LEAVING POSITIVE FEEDBACK

Good communication is the best strategy when using eBay and more often than not, you will have a very positive experience. If you receive your Corgi car on time, as described and with the politeness expected, you must leave positive feedback. It is what makes the wheels turn. Think extremely carefully before leaving negative comments as it sticks and is equally difficult to undo later on. Leaving positive feedback is a must if you got what you paid for.

7

OTHER PLACES TO BUY

THIS PART OF the book would not be complete without considering the joys of several other cheaper routes to making a mint. Don't forget your local charity shops, church fairs, school fairs and local ads. This is a secret weapon! This information can be added to your arsenal of buying skills and used whenever and wherever the opportunity presents itself.

CHARITY SHOPS

Often overlooked these days but still laden with goodies is the charity shop. I used to raid these for vintage clothes when I went through my 1950s phase. I also was lucky enough to pick up all manner of items from the past that I kept and used. Occasionally, if I had the time, I would also pop by whenever the possibility presented itself – just to scan the shelves for first edition books, nice and sellable crockery and the like.

In the last few years, some of the larger chains have cottoned on (and this can only be a good thing for the charities). They have special workers who are generalist experts who inspect the items left for them or answer calls from shop-floor staff to help sift the heavy hitters from the less valuable donations. Often the better pieces will be placed by the charity on eBay, or displayed in special locked cabinets and priced accordingly. This is really part of the overall trend in the UK of awareness of the market for collectables – something that has adversely affected the antiques business according to many professional dealers I meet when out and about filming.

Where this has come from is not crystal clear, but the proliferation of price guides, TV shows, eBay and investment potential has all been in play at some point or other.

Generally, the further away you go from a major city, the greater the chance of bagging yourself a bargain. That's a rule and there are plenty of exceptions. To be clear: you are more likely to find overlooked antiques, collectables and memorabilia in charity shops in the more remote towns and villages of the UK.

Many of the same buying tips come into play at car-boot fairs. You have less competition and more time to browse of course, but a shop will lack the huge array of objects and as we have established, the shop owners may have a checking system for new stock.

LOCATION, LOCATION, LOCATION

A golden tip that I am going to share with you now is something that will probably make you think 'Well, that's obvious,' but it is something you would only really do if you were truly committed to making mint. Here we go ...

Get a map of your region and pinpoint, with some Internet research, the posh neighborhoods! Make sure you are steering clear of the big cities and towns. For a short period, I went to school in a small town in Surrey. It was unfeasibly posh (I got a scholarship which covered the fees by the way!). The houses were enormous and the folk just plain wealthy. They also had incredibly good taste, to be frank.

The charity shops were therefore of a much, much better standard than my local and more rough and ready stomping ground. If you have the time, always stop by the local charity shops when holidaying away in nice little seaside towns or country villages. There is a better than average chance that the stuff for sale here will be cheap and of greater value.

Buy wisely; sell on elsewhere and everybody wins.

MORALS?

What happens if you come across, let's say, a genuine first edition copy of Philip Pullman's *Northern Lights* – a great book, in the BBC Big Read top three reads and now worth £4,000–6,000 if in very good shape or better? I have indeed seen a copy on the Internet a few years ago from a charity shop who knew the true value. Let's say you find a copy and it is 50 pence. Let's say you have read my chapter on identifying rare modern first edition books, and you buy it fair and square.

That is business after all.

Well, the truth is, I would take a step back and think about it for a moment. The charity shop is losing out on £4,000-6,000. That's a lot of money to anyone, but so much money to the charity.

All I can say is that you should seriously consider offering an anonymous donation of some value. It would be the ultra fair and ultra decent thing to do. I'd like to think that if I had that level of good fortune, I would share the proceeds with the charity.

Wouldn't you?

SCHOOL AND CHURCH FAIRS

Another route to making a mint is the largely unexplored territory of the school and church fairs. I used to buy toys from my sister's annual school fair when I was a nipper. In fact, I purchased a really cracking

Japanese robot that was boxed too. Alas, like so many toys, it was played with! Anyway, if I had kept it in good shape, it would be worth good money today.

Again, the same golden secret applies as above – use the Internet to find the posh schools in the posh areas. You are very unlikely to face stiff, if any competition from other professional dealers or collectors as most don't have the time to focus on a such niche area for picking up stock or new additions.

If you collect Corgi toys from the 1960s, you are wasting your time, aren't you really? However, if you are genned-up and hopefully fired-up by my information on the types of good collectables out there, which you'll read about in the third part of the book, you should be in possession of a knowledge base that it's 75% more developed than the average citizen!

- As with car-boot fairs, take your own laundry bags with bubble wrap or newspapers if necessary. Get there early and arrive with a bum bag full of change.
- Try and cover two or three sales over a weekend as they are often clustered together at Christmas, end of school terms or around the summer fête point at the close of the summer terms.
- Remember that private schools often have different term dates than the state sector.

DON'T LET BUYING OPPORTUNITIES PASS YOU BY!

I passed a village fête in a glorious West Country village last weekend. It was taking place on the central village green and was a glorious day for it. Sadly, it was midday and I was on a sports motorbike with a pillion – so very little chance of getting anything all the way back home.

I actually passed the same place on two days over two rides. If I had been smarter I would have packed a small rucksack, stopped and taken a look at the few stalls laid out with household clutter. With hindsight, it was a missed opportunity, so don't make the same mistake yourself. Village and summer fêtes could be a lovely way to pick up potential powersellers!

LOCAL ADS

An obvious place to investigate, but these days surprisingly overlooked I suspect. I used to do some presenting on a regional ITV show called *Trade It!* It was a commercial tie-in with my city's free ads paper. Though eBay was up and running, for most, the online auction site was unheard of back in 2000. eBay is of course a vast, international local paper in terms of buying potential and has the benefit of offering a better description – and a picture too.

Local ad papers also offer photos in some categories such as motor vehicles and many have an online element too. By and large, the sort of collectables we would be scouting for will not carry a picture and will have a short one- or two-line description only.

I know from 300-500 letters a week at the *Sunday Mirror* that it usually takes a couple of paragraphs to effectively describe an item (and two or three pictures to be sure). Local ad papers will require a beady eye and a willingness to phone up the seller to ask for more information.

Let's imagine you have spotted a listing for a vintage Bush radio. Well, that could easily be mis-described in the first place, as people have different opinions about what constitutes vintage and indeed, many old radio manufacturers have bought out immaculate FM reproductions in recent years. I would suggest asking upfront how long they have had it. Ask for a model number and a condition report. Quickly get the low-down and then establish if it is a vintage DAC 90, for example, and worth £90– 150 (depending on the colour of the cabinet). If it is a mini-treasure go and pick it up.

Don't forget to check the condition of the item first before parting with your cash. If the item is damaged, then tell them clearly that it needs some work to bring it up to scratch and offer half the asking price. I have found that if you don't ask, you absolutely will not get.

CHARITY SALES

I have been to quite a few… and hosted or auctioned at a load of them as well. If you are quick off the mark you can make a mint from celebrity hand-me-downs. There are plenty of charity auctions, some less publicised than others.

Prices can sometimes be high (reflecting the good cause and amount of wine consumed). Other times there is nobody interested in a particular lot for whatever reason and the prices are low. Some charity sales fly under the publicity radar so few people turn up and you can easily win the lots you are after.

One well-publicised charity sale took place in the summer of 2000 helped along by eBay.co.uk. It was organised to raise money for Breast Cancer Research and the lots were all handbags. The twist was that these were celebrity-owned items donated by stars including the PM's wife, barrister Cherie Booth, model Jerry Hall and Susannah and Trinny from BBC Television. The star item was Margaret Thatcher's black Ferragamo bag that was used throughout the 1980s while she was in office. This was auctioned with a hand-written letter of authenticity and it went on to make a record breaking £100,000!

You tend to get a real mixture of folk at charity auctions. Take for example my recent visit to the Corgi 50th anniversary celebration party. I was judging (and hosting) the worldwide Ultimate Collector

Competition. Just before my presentation, we held an auction of some incredibly rare Corgi collectables. In the audience were some members of the press, employees of Corgi, some former employees and a group of collectors. Two guesses who were the lucky bidders...

It was a wonderful opportunity for these passionate people to get some seriously exclusive purchases. They may add them to their collections or trade them... or they might make a profit if they later offer them to the world through an online auction. Either way, together with a balloon race, we raised a mighty £3,120 for Barnardo's in just a few hours. Everyone wins at charity sales.

Where to Find out More
- Barnardo's support children, young people and their families. If you would like to find out more about the charity and the work they do you can visit www.barnardos.org.uk.
- You can get lots of information about Corgi and the 50th anniversary year celebrations at www.corgi.biz.

WHERE AND
HOW TO SELL

Making a very special sale! No, surely… © Jamie Breese

INTRODUCTION

NOW WE COME to the next big thing – selling! Nothing much can beat the warm, glowing feeling you get when you buy something and sell it on for a profit. Humans have been bartering since the dawn of man. These days, things can be incredibly sophisticated with the trading floor in the great exchanges to high-end banking. However, it is still the same thing. Supply, demand. Demand, supply.

In the following chapters I am going to tell you about some of the best places to go to sell, the pros and cons of each route and also some insider tips on navigating them to ensure the best chances of success.

One of the really grand things about trading collectables is the feeling of control over your life. There are of course uncertainties, but nothing in life is guaranteed. A job for life rarely applies to anybody in modern Britain these days, and I for one love the feeling of control you get as a freelance – a solider who can be hired for any occasion. You can go where you please and go where the money is.

Collecting and selling antiques and collectables has changed quite a bit in the last decade. At the time of writing, there were 15 million registered users of eBay in the UK. Yes – just in the UK. For some, earning extra income or indeed making ones living is now possible with ones slippers on. There are folks who only ever buy and sell on eBay. I personally don't like the idea of being attached to a computer for most of my working hours… though I have been for a good few months writing this book! I make television programmes away from home frequently and that keeps me up to date with the business too.

I urge you to give all this a whirl. You may find it is not for you, but then again, it could open up a whole new chapter in your life and those of your family too. You do need some time and you also need to carefully consider your personal tax situation. You will need to visit the tax office website or give them a call to ensure you are keeping up with the paperwork as earnings are earnings whichever way you look at it, and the tax man will want to know. Get it right from the start and simply ask.

Before you read on, here's a tip. If you spend a few minutes cleaning anything that you plan to sell, you are doing something that most people don't bother to do. I used to buy lovely old leather suitcases from the 1920s to the 1950s. I got them for £2 at car-boot fairs as a boy. I would take them home, plonk them on some old newspaper and clean with saddle soap. I would then rub them down with dark tan polish from Kiwi and then polish the lovely but dirty brass locks with very fine wire wool, and lastly, the wonder product – Brasso. By spending 15 minutes on each item, I was able to sell them on for good money, and occasionally as much as £100.

Before you sell anything, spend a moment cleaning it up: that is one of the essential ways to really make a mint.

8

SELLING AT
CAR-BOOT FAIRS

I GOT THE car-booting bug very early on and have been involved since I was a teenager. It was in the early eighties that the phenomenon of the fair started to develop into the nationwide weekend pastime and business of today, most probably linked to the recession of that era.

Almost all my stock for my unit at Camden Stables Market would come from car boots around London. There followed a break from selling, then in March 2003, I started to co-present BBC2's *The Life Laundry* and I found myself filming at a different car boot sale each Sunday across the nation for nearly five straight months. It was a great experience and reminded me of where it all started. Effectively, each week I spent four days clearing out somebody's house and we would turn up at six in the morning with a huge truckload of clutter, some of it quite tasty. The cameras would roll and I would get selling.

THE PROS OF SELLING AT CAR-BOOT SALES

- The fair has truly become a national institution and a vital part of the recycling process. It is so often heard, but is so completely true – 'One man's trash is another man's treasure.'

- Many car-boot fairs manage to run throughout the year. The majority of events take place outdoors from Easter time onwards.
- It's a superb day out and a neat way to earn some extra cash.
- Low seller fee – usually the bigger the vehicle you have, the higher the cost, but £5-15 is quite normal.
- You get a first look at other sellers' stock. If you like to buy as well, then you are in the position to make your neighbour an offer before the punters arrive.
- You can shift items you have bought in job lots that you don't want or you can let go of your own household clutter. It will go if you play your cards right and the weather stays fine.
- If you are clearing a friend's or relative's house – here's the place to move on the dozens of smaller low-value pieces.

THE CONS OF SELLING AT CAR-BOOT FAIRS
- A key point to make is obvious: if you have something you know, or think might be precious, the car-boot fair is the least appropriate route for selling: better try the auction or Internet route with a more specialist group of people to present to.
- You need wheels and a day spare at the weekend.
- Many car-boot fairs are weather dependent.

THERE'S A GREAT BUZZ TO CAR-BOOTING!
When you're selling, there is the added benefit of being able to take a gander around the other stalls and hopefully pick up some bargains. The vast majority of sellers are there to de-clutter, but you'll be amazed at how many will return with a number of freshly picked pieces! So, let me take this opportunity to pass on some tips and tricks all about selling.

PREPARATION AND PRESENTATION

If you are a seasoned car-booter, then you may well be familiar with some of these points. If not, take heed and make sure you cover your bases. It's a fun but sometimes fast-moving adventure and you need to be well prepared.

• Take a look through those cluttered cupboards, attic spaces and garages and get tough on yourself: be ruthless. Set yourself a time limit and stick to it.

• Box and pack up items by type. Clearly label each box to make setting up quick and easy on the day.

• If you have a feeling that something may be valuable, put it in a clearly labelled box and have a look at the items covered in more detail later on in this book. Still unsure whether you should take them to the car boot? Then why not pay a visit to your local auction house for a valuation. A call beforehand can save a journey if in doubt.

• Get organised! Buy some price labels from the stationery shop and label everything that you intend to sell. This is not always the norm, but I have found some buyers are put off by unlabelled goods and are not all are confident enough to ask the price – this might lose you sales. A good compromise is a colour-coding system using stickers – you know what price bracket items are in on the day.

• Everyone and their auntie will ask for a price cut so do not forget to include some leeway in your pricing.

• Bring a friend or family member to help out. It's hard graft on your own.

ESSENTIAL KIT

I cannot do a fair without at least two trestle or pasting tables. You can usually pick them up for under £20 at DIY stores. Yes, it's an outlay upfront, but if you can't borrow one from a friend, then you need to take the plunge. Alternatively, a piece of chipboard laid across four milk crates can suffice as long as you cover it with a tablecloth or blanket. That brings me to another point: make sure you think about presentation.

- Keep books and records in one place (away from the front of stall).
- Try and borrow a clothes rail – these are absolutely brilliant and save a lot of hassle on the day – for you and the punters.
- Keep the more pricey ornaments within arms' (and eyes') reach on the table in front. Jewellery, coins and medals sell well if fixed to a cushion.
- Make sure you bring a chair too – the day's a long one in the summer. And forget fashion – ultra comfortable footwear is a must.
- Prepare your food the night before. You can end up queuing in the morning and lose valuable set-up time. There is usually catering at most fairs and it has to be said, nothing beats a bacon buttie at 6am!
- Packaging is important: don't bother with expensive bubble wrap. Instead, take along lots of old newspapers and carrier bags. It's good customer PR to pack well.
- Along with the goods, the next most important thing is a moneybag, bumbag or money-belt. Prepare plenty of change. Do not underestimate how much you will need from the minute you drive in.
- If you have any doubts about the safety of your goods, do not sell them!

JAMIE'S TOP TIPS

At certain fairs, especially in cities, you need to be prepared beforehand for the early stampede of professional antique dealers, other sellers and general public.

I have attended some events where cars are swooped on by dealers as they arrive, before you've even opened up the boot. Sometimes I'll just say, 'Sorry, nothing being sold for 15 minutes' and stick by it, otherwise you never get set up. Some sellers just go off for a cup of tea for 15 minutes and wait for the dealers to move elsewhere.

INDIVIDUAL OR TRADER

There are legal implications to both:

- If you are hiring anybody to help you or sell the same stuff from home, then you are a trader.
- Are the items you are selling your own property? If not, and you are buying in items to sell, then you are more than likely to be a trader in British law.
- Are you selling at car-boot sales frequently? This could be classed as trading.
- If you actually are a trader, then you have to abide by various laws including The Price Marking Order, The Consumer Protection Act and The Sale and Supply of Goods Act.
- If you are not a trader (more than likely if you are reading this), then you should avoid selling electrical goods such as kettles
and toasters. Children's clothes and toys should also be checked
by you to ensure there are no hazards, particularly with older
items. Child car seats and other safety items like crash helmets

should never be sold on. Trading Standards can advise on the latest rules and regulations.

- You are still bound to describe your goods accurately and offer a refund if you are clearly in the wrong after the sale.
- Check with your local trading standards for the latest position. You can find telephone numbers and addresses of the nearest office at www.tradingstandards.gov.uk.

ON THE DAY

Before setting off, it is worthwhile checking the weather. If you have a contact number, phone the organizers as they sometimes leave a recorded message with an update. If it is going to be very bad all day, I'd urge you to pass, unless it is a covered event. Muddy fields are not ideal for selling, your car might get stuck in the mud and there's likely to be fewer punters.

Think carefully about what you're going to wear. Wrap up warm, even in the summer because most car boots start early (usually between 6 and 8am) and it can be extremely chilly in these often huge open spaces. It's best to take lots of layers, and don't forget a sun hat and sunscreen too. As we all found on *The Life Laundry*, you need to take plenty of water.

Even before you get there, think about your exit strategy. The ends of aisles are best when it comes to your departure. There are no particular rules about when you can stay until, but be warned that it can be difficult to slip away too early, especially if you're in the middle of a row.

I would often be a bit proactive when it comes to flogging the goods. This would involve gentle banter and later, more vocal hawking and pleading. At the end of the day, you want to shift as much as you can, so in the final hour consider striking better deals and announcing that

Everything Must Go! I would make the most money in this last hour usually as a result of straining my vocal chords.

JAMIE'S TOP TIP

The early bird – you must arrive early! The best pitches are the ones near the entrance, or near to catering vehicles (as you have more people in the vicinity).

My strategy is to be polite and humorous at all times. It's not life and death and you are usually dealing with small amounts. Be honest about goods and if they work or not. Do not sell faulty electrical goods! Similarly, make friends with your neighbours – they're useful for providing change and information about other boot sales worth doing. They might even watch your stall if you have to nip to the loo.

Lastly, if you are left with plenty of stock and are not planning a return visit in the near future, then I suggest looking about for a few of the more regular traders and offering a job lot at a knockdown price just to get shot of it. You can always pay a visit to your local charity shop on the way back.

Where to Find out More

The *Car Boot Calendar* is the industry guidebook to most of the fairs around the country. You can visit their website at www.carbootcalendar.com or phone the office on 01981 251 633.

When I presented *The Antiques Show* on BBC2 back in 1999, I was interviewed by the Car Boot Calendar, the UK's leading listings guide.

CBC: I understand your parents are antique dealers. Did they encourage you to get to know the business?

JB: Absolutely! My folks have done a stall at Portobello Road since the early 1980s. My stepmother has dealt in ephemera (paper collectables such as luggage and cigar labels etc.), all her life. I found myself helping out at the stall at weekends and caught the bug early on. I have to say, I was the only youngster around and got exposed to the incredible characters who occupy the antiques world. Like my folks, they often have completely different weekday jobs and operate their stall because of their passion for buying, selling and handling antiques and collectables.

I decided to break out on my own, following in the footsteps of a buddy who has stayed in the game. I rented a space at a unit in the stables market at Camden and set up stall there. These years were probably the most exciting of my life – you never earn a fortune but the money which comes your way feels very special, because you know that every single penny was earned through your own hard graft. Much like the buzz of selling at a car boot (which I've also done). Operating a stall is a great way to develop solid business acumen and it taught me a lot about life.

CBC: How did you first become interested in car-boot sales?

JB: It was out of necessity really as I had to find the stock for my dealing. The highlight of the week quickly became the multiple visits to the sales and the CBC was invaluable. Ironically I couldn't drive, so I bought and restored a 1950s postman's bicycle and spent my days wobbling around London, dangerously overloaded with stock, precariously balancing on any part of me that protruded!

Oh yes, and I occasionally pressganged my mum into bringing her Mini into battle. London is well sorted for car boots so it's not difficult to get stock. My favourite fairs were in Kilburn and the market car park at Shepherd's Bush – both were close, with other fairs dotted around nearby.

CBC: What age were you when you first started buying and selling and what did you concentrate on?

JB: The buzz of the car boot is something I think everyone shares. I think I caught it in my early teens. I would tear around scanning the stalls, looking like a Terminator, zooming in and out if I saw something tasty. It really is like going on a treasure hunt! Sometimes I'd run, sometimes I'd dress down, to avoid looking like I had much cash – the stories are endless.

I was looking primarily for twentieth-century collectables. Things I knew I could spend a little time on with some Brasso and a little TLC and turn into something that someone would snap up from my stall. Leather luggage was a favourite, as were chrome items from the 30s, 40s and 50s. I would buy Goblin teasmades and ice skates, soda-siphons and Art Deco porcelain. Anything Bakelite and so on.

CBC: What was the first real bargain that you bought – the one item that made you think 'I can do this'?

JB: I think it was probably an old black Bakelite telephone – the ones made by Ericsson in the late 30s and early 40s. It had a cheese drawer and cloth cable and was in fine condition. I had seen my friend sell his phones for around a ton and snapped it up for a couple of quid. They are beautiful objects and part of our nation's cultural history. For me, that was the real appeal of the business – something which not only had character and style, but something which people actually used and through me (with a little tinkering) could go away and start using all over again. The coloured Bakelite telephones are the Holy Grails. Chinese red was for the fire service, green was for the civil service and there is even a rumour of a Royal blue, made for the monarchy.

CBC: And what is the best ever bargain from a car boot?

JB: There are so many to quote from. My friend, Mr G, recently picked up a quirky tribal mask for £7 at a car boot in West London. He hung it up and there it stayed… until the day he saw one adorning the front of an auction catalogue. His find later commanded £7,000!

A Bristol woman bought a damaged clay ornament 'with wavy lines' for £3.50. It turned out to be a priceless, 5000-year-old Predynastic Egyptian pot! A man paid a hefty £50 for an eighteenth-century porcelain dessert service. Most of it was then sold on to my colleague at *The Antiques Roadshow*… for £95,000!

CBC: You then moved on to antique dealing. Do car-boot sales figure in the antiques world?

JB: I would say that they are an important part of the business. They allow everyone – dealer or not, to have a crack of the whip. I remember a boy who would do the West London fairs. He was about nine, maybe ten at the outside, on his own and always there. He would steam around the sales, looking like a man (boy) possessed, and just pushed and slipped his way to the front and pushed his hands around inside the trays. He was an expert in jewellery. Lord knows what he's doing now – but I bet he's got a shop and I also bet he still does the car-boot sales! For me, car boots were the main source of my stock. Everyone won, nobody lost and after my repairs, some lucky tourist would have something to take away with them to remind them of Blighty.

CBC: There is some criticism of car-boot sales in that they are supposedly a marketplace for stolen and contraband goods. Stallholders are said to be earning thousands per week without paying taxes and so on. What's your take on that?

JB: Let me put my cards on the table. I am pro car boots. Simply because they offer something to everyone. The myths about criminality and dodgy goods are just that – myths. I don't think I've ever come across any shenanigans. Car booters are honest, hard working people. There is no such thing as career for life – jobs aren't easy to come by. Anyway, I don't recollect anyone grumbling about trading through classifieds or ads in shop windows. What's the difference? It's all small-scale stuff and allows people who are on low incomes to find items that would normally cost them their weekly take home.

CBC: So on the whole you think car-boot sales are a good thing? Why do you think they are so successful?

JB: I think car-boot sales are an important part of the life of the British people. As I said, they offer something to everyone – families, collectors, enthusiasts and young antique hunters. Two to three million people can't be wrong. They also play an important part in this country's recycling process. Stuff which would otherwise get chucked ends up being re-used and admired once again. Many events now have a first aid point, larger fairs also have an electrical testing point and sometimes organised security to make sure everything goes smoothly –

watching the car parks, preventing queue jumping and so on. Oh, and by the way, spending a day at a car-boot sale is also good fun.

CBC: Any tips to our readers as to how to buy successfully?

JB: Where do you start? Buy with your eyes. Spending your own money sharpens them; take lots of change in a moneybelt for easy access; get there early if possible, though some of my best finds have been at the end of the day; don't bother to pay by cheque or card; take a big laundry bag with you; move quickly from stall to stall; always haggle but never be pushy; don't be too clever and give the seller some respect (and credit); don't look or talk like an antiques dealer or expert as you might pay more; buy items with potential for future collectability such as early boxed or mint electronics, mobiles, toys, any limited-edition stuff, first-edition books, anything unique (a painting which is signed, for example, or a mis-casting of a toy); dress up warmly; bring the kids – and have fun.

Reprinted with kind permission of *The Car Boot Calendar*

9

SELLING AT HOME

BACK IN 2002 I had the good fortune to find myself involved in a brand new television show called *Everything Must Go!* It was one of those calls you get completely out of the blue and most welcome!

The show was to begin filming in a few day's time and I would have to drop everything for a good few months to make the commitment. It was to go out on the early afternoon slot on ITV1. From what I could gather, the show was about families who were selling up and moving on. My co-presenter and I would not only be hosting the show, but were set to rummage through their possessions and dig out interesting pieces to tell the folks at home about. In addition, we were to value practically everything they owned for a house sale! Now, this is still quite uncommon in Britain. In the US, they are called garage sales and are more popular.

In short, we were going to advertise the house sale through the local press, radio and TV and invite locals to come along and snap up a bargain at the house. This all sounded rather risky. Would the house owners have anything worth buying? Would anybody ever show up? Would we ever find anybody mad enough to let us and a few million viewers, let alone the public off the street, into their homes?

It all seemed a bit crazy but as luck would have it, it all fitted into place. The lure of the camera helped draw in some curious buyers for sure, but in general, folks just turned up because they were looking for a bargain. We found that over the series, and then several other series, the best sales and best turn ups in terms of punters were in the smaller towns. Word of mouth was just excellent. The big cities like Birmingham and London attracted fewer buyers sadly.

TRUST ME, I KNOW WHAT I'M TALKING ABOUT

The series ran and ran over the years. I had a few different co-presenters too. It even developed into a spin-off series called *Everything Must Go! Under the Hammer*. Here, we solved one of the problems of series one: what do we do with the real antiques of value? In this show, we took the best items off to auction and sold them there. It was great fun and at the time, ground-breaking for daytime television and the genre. We were there before *Cash in the Attic* and similar shows.

So, after hundreds of episodes, you could say I have got rather used to the format and certainly have developed a set of skills for helping to hold the perfect house sale. I don't say that to impress you, but to impress upon you that I have simply got years of experience, and have held and overseen more house sales than anybody else. What I am going to share with you are the best pointers to holding a house sale in your community. I would recommend this route to selling if you live in a large town or smaller.

THE PROS OF SELLING AT HOUSE SALES

- It doesn't take a lot of organisation.
- Items, when sold, are removed by the buyers and at their cost.
- Smaller items such as lampshades, cutlery and the like always shift.

- If well promoted, you can expect to sell up to 75% of your stock.
- This is ideal if you are moving house, moving country or downsizing to a smaller place.
- You make money, and quickly.
- There are no substantial start-up costs and only a few quid is required to place ads in shop windows. All other selling routes have inherent costs whether it be eBay or car boots.
- It is great fun if approached correctly and planned well.

THE CONS OF SELLING AT HOUSE SALES

- You are inviting Joe Public into your very own home. This is clearly not for everyone.
- Be aware that in three years of house sales, only one item I knew about got pinched – an electric toothbrush. Whether the camera put light fingers off or not is not clear.
- It is not the best route to take if you have plenty of rare collectables, delicate and pricey ornaments or bulky antiques. Check later collectables chapters to see if you have the sort of things that might fit into this bracket.
- It will take a day to prepare, your friends' and family's assistance and a day to put the house back in order.

PLANNING FOR THE SALE

You are the boss on this occasion and are answerable to yourself only. That's a great thing. It also carries certain responsibilities in terms of paying attention to the health and safety of your punters. More on that later.

So, you have decided to have a house sale. Firstly, you need to pick a day. Find one when you are free for the day before and the day after. Just as important, pick a day when at least six of your friends and family are too. They will be asked to work in pairs.

Set a date in your diaries and stick to it. There is a big deal of truth in the expression 'if you schedule something, you make it a reality'.

Choose a start time of around 1.30pm. That always worked for us quite well – before school pick-ups in the late afternoon, but after lunch. Plan on closing up by 6.30pm.

> **JAMIE'S TOP TIP**
>
> Talk to your house insurers – you are likely to need extra insurance when you allow Joe Public into your home.

WHAT HAVE YOU GOT TO SELL?

So, you have talked your friends into helping out. Great. Next up is one of the tricky ones. What have you got? I would firstly take a good hard look around the house, garden and garage. Use your own judgement to identify the clear or potential 'big ticket' items. I would suggest buying some red, orange and white stickers from your local office supply shop and marking up items with all three colours in the week leading up to the sale.

Red is not for house sale. Orange is to remind yourself to check the possible value. White is for the price tags. Clearly, for anything that looks like an antique or more collectable, you should do a bit of research.

The Second Part of this Book

Here you will find a substantial overview of some of the key collectables and valuable objects of the twentieth century. Use this as a guide to making informed decisions about which items to sell elsewhere.

Internet Search

Use a good search engine such as Google and place your keywords in quotation marks to narrow down the search to the exact item. You should get a good idea on many items by doing this, but it can take hours if you have a good deal of orange-tagged items.

Reference Books

I have a good library of reference books because it is my job to know. However, you'd be surprised to learn that almost every home I have sifted through the years has had a copy of one of the hardback price guides such as the *Miller's* guides.

Your local library is a great place to browse for values, but again, like all books, chances are that many of the current values are simply out of date. Often by years! However, they will still tell you if your object is likely to be desirable if the price was once high – at least you'll know to make orange items red.

eBay

There is an online price guide out there to scour for free. I tend to go on a mixture of eBay 'Buy It Now' prices and the end results of auctions. One could argue that the worldwide reach of this powerful player means that the prices achieved are often quite reliable indicators. Go check it out.

> **JAMIE'S TOP TIP**
> - Think about what to do if it rains.
> - Warn your neighbours.

ADVERTISING

You must make sure you get the buyers on the day. I must confess that during filming there were at least three occasions when, for whatever reason, we had a terrible turn out. Nobody knew why and it remains a mystery to this day. I remember presenting the opening link to the second half of the show, immediately preceding the cutting of the ribbon. Normally by this stage, we have wandered up and down the line of several hundred punters – chatting, teasing and asking what sort of things they are looking for – and usually getting some great snippets for the show called vox pops.

There was nobody – I think maybe three or four people! I excitedly ran my usual patter, 'Everything Must Go! Including this presenter' as I pretended to walk off with my tail between my legs. It was a sight.

So you want to do everything you can to avoid that. You will have a small disadvantage in that you don't have the power of two dedicated TV researchers behind you: it is normally their job to promote the sale on the local radio and press beforehand. We also gave out flyers on the local high street the morning of the sale. It counts for a lot when you have the ITV logo on a flyer. However, this disadvantage can also be seen as a definite advantage too! I believe it is offset by the same very fact: a surprising number of people do not want to be on national television. It's true.

My Top Three Suggestions for Getting Punters In

1. Hand out printed flyers with the date and time, address and a hint of the types of bargains to be had. Hand these out in your local high street the week preceding the sale, as well as that morning.

2. Contact your local press. You would be surprised at how supportive they are, especially if you have some type of unique selling point. Perhaps you are selling up to move to a foreign destination and have been a member of the community for years, or maybe you are donating 10% of all your proceeds to the local hospice.

   Anything newsworthy should be relayed to them and hopefully they will send a photographer. Hell, why not say you are doing your very own *Everything Must Go!* It all makes for interesting copy and then all they need to do is add the sale date and time.

3. Don't forget posters in local shop windows. This works well, particularly in communities that have a local focal point such as a post office, pub or newsagent.

PRACTICAL PREPARATION

Get your home ready the day before. Here are the basics:

- The day before the sale, use yellow striped 'safety' gaffer tape to secure any loose carpet or uneven surfaces in your home.
- Go out and buy some very cheap carpet off-cuts or tiles from an old exhibition and cover the key walkways in and out of the house. Use the same gaffer tape to secure these coverings so folks don't go flying.
- While you are at it, collect as many carrier bags and old newspapers as possible from friends and neighbours.
- Prepare at least four moneybelts with change – plenty of.

- Print and put up disclaimer signs – things are bought as seen and you won't have liability.
- Mare sure you have a lockable safety box to keep cash as it builds up.
- Buy five or six bright red or yellow oversize T-shirts from the pound shop. These act as your organisers' identity badges – so punters know who to come and haggle with.
- Keep one or two rooms as out of bounds. Print up a few signs on A4 and tack them to the doorways. Use these rooms to place key RED items and personal possessions. If the room locks, then better still.
- Got a garden? Then use it. If it is not likely to rain, hustle a friend for the loan of a mini marquee. While you're at it, track down as many trestle or pasting tables as you can.
- Pricing up. This is not a car-boot sale and you are not overseeing every transaction. You need to give yourself a break (and your helpers a hand) by pricing up each and every item for sale.
- Prices – set each price at 25% more than you are hoping to get. Everybody will haggle and this is part of the fun.
- In each room, ensure that the newspapers and carrier bags you sourced earlier are in easy-to-reach boxes.
- If you or your friends happen to have a couple of walkie-talkies, then grab them and check the batteries. They are great for communicating from house to garden to check prices with you if uncertainty arises or a price sticker goes missing.

JAMIE'S TOP TIP

Layout is important. Keep books and records in easy-to-browse cardboard boxes. Keep these well out of the way of the front of the tables as punters often spent a great deal of time thumbing through these. Keep ornaments and delicate objects on nicely covered, flat and stable surfaces.

ON THE DAY
Motivate Your Troops

- The private room signs should be up and the doors locked where possible.
- Hopefully, by around 1pm, you will have a healthy queue out there on the pavement.
- Don't be tempted to let anybody in – therein lies the way to potential hostility from those who are true bargain hunters.
- Keep one helper at the front door to keep the crowd in the loop. They should also stick around there to check that nobody is taking away unpaid-for items – i.e. pinching anything! This is less likely in my experience, but the presence of a helper is a natural deterrent.
- Gather your helpers around. You should all have your T-shirts on and moneybelts at the ready.
- Helpers should always be in pairs in the larger rooms – one to pack and one to haggle and take money.
- For heaven's sake, make sure they know which items are the potential star sellers – otherwise they won't be friends for much longer!
- Remind your helpers to check if in real doubt and to be polite and

firm when it comes to handling pushy punters or excessive, rude haggling.

- Thank them all for the time they are giving.

JAMIE'S TOP TIP

Remind everyone of the pricing system: everything is marked up by 25 per cent of what you are hoping to take. Tell them to use their own discretion when it comes to going any lower. Often, towards the end of the sale, you should consider taking 50 per cent off the price tag – just to get shot of the stuff.

Open the Sale!

The fun begins. On a good day, I have always found that the initial 30 minutes or so is the most frantic. You simply can't keep up with it all in that time period. It will always start to thin out after the first dash.

Half-time Check-up

At about 4pm, take a moment to go around the house and speak to your helpers. Discuss how things are going, what the big sales have been and give each of your helpers a tea and loo break.

Do you need to keep pushing on? Yes! Unless it is absolutely dead and has been for a while, you need to keep on trucking as 5.30pm to 6.30pm often brings other family members, folks who've heard about it through word of mouth and those from offices who are willing to stop by and take a gander.

At around 5.30pm, you should also decide whether you want a clear house at the end, or are willing to horde the leftovers for an eBay sale or charity shop drop-off. It's your call, but in my mind, you started something, so you might as well finish it! If you are ready to let go of everything, tell your helpers to lower their price levels, offer three for ones, and take what they can.

Wrapping Up

When 6.30pm comes, take a moment to put the kettle on for everybody. Get together to see what is left and tot up the cash.

Consider donating a few leftover pieces to your helpers as a goodwill gesture and perhaps look at dropping off the remainder at the local hospice or charity shop if you feel you can live without it all and are sure they are not of any great value.

10

SELLING AT AUCTION

AUCTIONS HAVE BECOME second nature to me. It started when I was a teenager and into my early twenties. My interest was fired up again when I started in television in the late 1990s. I did a few shows for regional TV and then I found myself presenting a show with none other than the legendary Judith Miller at an auction house in Dorset. It was called the *Antiques Trail* and was a clever concept. Judith and the late Ross Benson were the presenters. Essentially, they had the job of tracking an object from place to place – never quite knowing where it would end up. I joined them for a few shows as a young sidekick and had a great time.

A couple of years later, I was fronting *Everything Must Go!* After series one, we knew we had to find an outlet to sell the real antiques and collectables. The team dreamt up the show *Everything Must Go! Under the Hammer*. Practically every day, I found myself filming the viewings and the sales themselves, at not just one, but dozens of different auction houses all over the country. You quickly get to develop a keen eye for trends and, of course, you sharpen all those skills when helping other people to make the most of their items.

In the following pages I am going to share the best information I have with you.

HISTORY

In England, the first ever auctions took place in late 1400s but they can be traced back to Roman armies who would carve up their plunder by auction. After the Restoration in the mid 1600s, auctions became much more commonplace. Covent Garden was one of the main centres of the business back then.

Their most enticing aspect is the chance to unearth 'sleepers', or potentially valuable hidden treasure among the boxes that often line the smaller salesrooms. That part is more about buying and I deal with that in the first part of this book.

As we have seen, there are two types of non-Internet auctions: specialist sales and general sales. Mostly I will be referring to general sales – but if you have something quite special, you will probably make more profit on it by waiting and sending it off to a specialist sale.

THE PROS OF SELLING AT AUCTION

- You can pass over the selling task to professionals who have years of experience.
- If you have a number of potential lots (items for sale), have little time or knowledge, then auctions can be a one-stop shop.
- A great place to sell specialist goods to a captive audience. Most items are listed in advance in catalogues and sometimes online.
- Buyers don't have to be present: telephone and Internet bidding is most common today.
- You get a free valuation service and advice and assistance in transport.

THE CONS OF AUCTIONS

- There are certain costs involved for the seller and the buyer.
- It can be a little daunting for the first-time seller as everyone seems to be in the know and talking their own jargon.

WHAT IS IT WORTH?

If you have just had a house sale, you may have a few orange and red sticker items left over, or you may have an item that you know absolutely nothing about but feel it could be worth a penny or two. Your local auction house is on hand.

FINDING AN AUCTION HOUSE

There is a salesroom in every corner of the land and you should have no difficulty finding one. If you think you have something that is clearly rather special, e.g. a match shirt worn by David Beckham, or an old rug from Iran, then you should consider a specialist sale. However, these often take place only once or twice a year – usually in the larger houses in major cities.

Other options include:

- *Collect-it!* magazine.
- *Antiques Info.*
- Your local paper often carries adverts.
- Word of mouth – just ask folks who have been there before.
- The Internet can yield quick results through a targeted search using a popular search engine such as google.co.uk or yahoo.co.uk.
- The *Antiques Trade Gazette.*

MEET THE EXPERT

Take your item along to the salesroom. It is preferable to call in advance, and with very particular items or collections as you may be able to arrange a visit by an expert. Most services such as this are free.

It is important that you try and give as much information as possible at this stage. All these clues help build up a quick picture. It is usually referred to as an item's provenance and just makes everyone's jobs a lot easier. If you have old receipts from when your mother bought it in the 1950s or an interesting story about how it was acquired, now is the time to tell.

Valuations do vary from place to place and, of course, country to country. One idea is to consider visiting a couple of auction houses to see how the land lies. The Internet is another obvious stopping point to get some factoids. Auctioneers are busy people, so do your prep first.

JAMIE'S TOP TIPS

One of the more common routes is asking the expert to evaluate your item by email. Many people have a camera phone these days and it is a doddle to send over a few clear pictures and a tight description. Sometimes an evaluation can be over the phone – it takes seconds to tell somebody that their 'Stradivarius' is actually one of the thousands of copies made in the East.

SET YOUR RESERVES

This is all very straightforward, but is a must. Use the information that the expert has provided and agree a reserve price for each lot. This is the lowest price that you will accept on the day. If an item is valued at £1,000, then you might gun for around £750 or so. Reserves are legally binding and must be respected by the auctioneer on the day.

ASK FOR THE RATES

There are certain costs involved as a vendor:

- Catalogue and advertising charges are often made. If your lot is featured in the auction catalogue, you might have to pay for the costs of photography and occasionally research to help better describe the item.

- 'Lottage' or a 'Lotting fee' is a smallish fee that is charged to place your item up for grabs at auction. Some auctions do not ask for this.

- Commission is the most familiar charge. Every auction house will charge it and this is all very standard. Rates do vary but somewhere between 10 and 15% is about right. This comes from the final 'hammer' price that the item sells for on the day of the sale. It has been known for vendors who have quite a few pieces to negotiate these rates. If you don't ask, you don't get.

- Don't forget, there is also VAT to pay on top of that commission.

- Other costs can come into play from time to time and you need to ask upfront. Sometimes handling fees or even insurance is required.

- Insurance is usually around 1%. Today, the Internet plays a big role in pre-sale publicity and there can be a fee for this too. Again, VAT will be added to those fees.

JAMIE'S TOP TIPS

If your lot fails to sell, there can be a charge. I have often simply rolled lots over into the next relevant sale and dropped the reserve a bit.

PAYMENT

Not always lightning fast but you will get your money. More often than not, it will take a few weeks, though some places turn it all around in a few days.

11

SELLING TO
A DEALER

HAVING BEEN A dealer in the past I am able to offer you an insider's point of view. Going this route is one of many ways to make a mint. The bottom line is that it is less likely to make you a profit unless you were left the object or obtained it cheaply from lower down in the food chain, from a charity shop or car boot sale, for example.

THE PROS OF SELLING TO A DEALER
- You are able to make an ultra quick sale with no hidden costs.
- If your collection or even single object is of enough interest, a dealer will travel to you, saving you time and money.
- If you are not computer savvy and want to avoid some of the possible pitfalls of online auctions, then this route could be for you.
- Unlike online auctions, you can deal with your buyer face to face and possibly strike up a long standing relationship if you can keep supplying similar wares.
- You can contact a trade association such as LAPADA or BADA who can recommend good dealers to contact.

- You have a degree of control in that you can offer to several dealers and check who pays more.

THE CONS OF SELLING TO A DEALER

This book is about making a mint. A dealer needs to make a profit. You should expect less than 'book' price (price guide suggestions) and sometimes under 50% of its value. It is business and nobody hides this fact.

- You generally have to start the ball rolling when it comes to negotiating. It is the seller's responsibility to set the initial asking price – the dealer can then say yes or no or make an offer based on that.
- You are dealing with a seasoned, possibly tough negotiator and expert salesperson too. You are unlikely to have the same level of experience. I am not talking about dishonesty here at all; I just mean there are all sorts of little techniques, like feigning disinterest, that somebody can use to beat down a price, as in many businesses.

PLACE TREASURE WITH THE TRASH

If you have a quantity of items, try and position the treasure among the trash and insist that the item is a 'job lot'. I once came back from an auction in Shepherd's Bush. In order to buy some neat vintage electric fans and radios, I had to take about 100 awful old household items from the 1960s and 70s. These were of no use to me, but a few of the items – a 1910 toaster among them – were likely to be of use to a local film and TV prop rental company so I used the same technique to pass the items up through the 'food chain'!

I had a domestic situation to deal with as well. My mother was absolutely hitting the roof, as she came back from work that evening and found the front room crammed with dusty bits of old metal. We are talking literally 'old irons', toasters and other bits of tat. It was a real sight and the atmosphere was genuinely tense.

I contacted the prop company, the guy turned up and he ended up picking only the items that he needed, rather than my initial goal of flogging the whole lot and being done with it. I didn't stick by my guns – I was just a kid, dealing with a pro buyer, and any money for this old rope was tempting. Even getting the chap to my house could have been a problem initially, but I loaded it in my favour. Fortunately I was able to lure him in with a 1930s television that I had bought privately at a low price earlier that week too, and for a modest profit.

Because he wasn't looking to resell, I got close to book price – therein lies a tip. Sell to prop companies, as they don't need to profit from re-sell in the same way. They milk the item over years and years and make their money that way. I was left with half of the unwanted stock but knew I could shift the remainder over a few visits to a car-boot fair. It all worked out okay and taught me some good lessons.

Jamie's Tips and Tricks

I would like to offer you a few tips and tricks for getting the most out of this route of selling:

1. A word of caution to those of you reading this for fun, rather than planning to go out and make a mint. It is strongly inadvisable to sell your possessions, especially antiques and collectables, to 'knockers' or individuals or groups who turn up unannounced to make an offer!

2. This happens less and less because of TV programmes revealing what goes on, but if you are vulnerable and living on your own you should be extra certain in your conviction when politely saying 'no thank you'. You simply will not get anywhere near the book price and anyway, you should never allow unexpected strangers into your home.

12

SELLING ON EBAY

EBAY IS OFFICIALLY king of the online auction world. It is a superb resource for people looking to make a mint and has encouraged the inner bargain hunter in us all to come out to play. For more information and an overview about eBay, I encourage you to take a look at my earlier chapters in this book that focuses on buying using eBay.

THE PROS OF SELLING ON EBAY

- Your very own shop front – located in a worldwide high street.
- Very low overheads compared to a shop and it is cheaper to sell. In many cases, cheaper than a good car-boot fair.
- Millions of customers online, in different time zones, at any given time.
- Relatively straightforward to sell.
- An auction in your living room – you don't have to travel to leave items at the auction room or worry about moving them if they are unsold.
- The buyer traditionally pays for the postage.
- Quick profit potential! You can buy cheap at your local Sunday car

boot, have it on eBay by lunchtime and sold for a profit –
sometimes huge – by suppertime!
- You can set reserve prices to ensure you get closer to what
you want.
- The *Buy It Now* and similar features can make for a much quicker
turnaround if you need to sell it mega quick.
- You can sell multiple items of a similar kind – a 'Dutch' auction –
and it is hassle free.
- In the UK there is a buyer and seller protection programme on
certain listings.
- The more you sell, the more credibility you gain: and unlike in the
real world, the buyer can see this! Keep clean and you are
considered a 'trustworthy' trader.
- The possibility of conducting all your selling via this route – maybe
even to up your game and become a 'Powerseller'. Some estimates
suggest that 20% of eBay's sales are people actually making a
business of it.
- eBay has an autoresponder system. This means that you, the seller,
do not need to be stuck next to your wares all day and night.
- The commissions (known as Final Value Fees) charged to sellers are
traditionally much less than the traditional auction house.

THE CONS OF SELLING ON EBAY
- Bad feedback can damage your chances of future trading.
- If a frequent seller, you need to spend time packing and posting.
- If you have no computer, or computer skills, you are not going to
be able to participate easily.
- The 'virtual reality' of this type of selling doesn't appeal to everyone.

- eBay performs best if you have a broadband connection to the Internet. If you have a dial-up connection it will be difficult.
- Though many important pieces have been sold this way, many feel the specialist auction rooms of a major city are better suited to big ticket wares including memorabilia, artworks and highly delicate items such as rugs and porcelain.
- There are all sorts of additional fees that a seller can be tempted to pay depending on the profile they would like to give their listing.

CELEBRITY SALES

I have sold some great pieces on eBay before and have a 100% positive feedback score I am pleased to say. I have even taken celebrities by the hand – from start to finish – through the eBay experience. On one show for BBC2 called *The Life Laundry*, I went to help DJ and Pop Quiz/Radio 1 legend Mike Reid clear out his clutter. I spent five days there! He had rooms and rooms full of boxes – and among these were some really great items.

For example, I sold a really valuable jukebox from the 1950s for him using eBay. It was valued at thousands of pounds. I sold loads of superb music memorabilia from Radio One Roadshow shirts to a one-off Mike Reid Action Man! eBay was the perfect route through which to sell because he was so well known and we had immediate access to millions of potential buyers who knew him and had grown up listening and watching this great man.

Two Important Suggestions

1. Focus on Collectables (and antiques if you know your onions).

   Most people start their eBay experience by selling unwanted clutter from their homes. This is great and forms the real backbone of the system. However, unless you live in a sprawling country estate, you are unlikely to Make a Mint! by doing this.

   I would suggest that you keep focused on an area that, firstly, holds your interest and secondly, that you have started to develop some knowledge on. I like rare books and I know the sort of authors to look for and how to identify a rare book (so will you when you read the chapter in my collectables section of this book).

2. Buy To Sell

   To be a successful seller, you also need to have at least gone through the buying process on one occasion so you can understand how it works and what a buyer expects to happen. If you don't get a grip of buying, you will probably have the misfortune of a bad experience and gain negative feedback – a huge turn-off for potential bidders in the future.

GETTING STARTED

Anybody can sell something using eBay. Here is my quick and easy guide to get cooking. Make sure you are registered first. It is thrilling when the first item sells and you await your first feedback. Aim to sell at least one item this week if you have not done it before.

WHAT HAVE YOU GOT?

I would suggest that if it is your first time you prepare a listing for something of low value which will sell quickly. Be prepared to even take a hit on it – namely, lose a small amount, just to get you into the game.

I have a speciality in collecting rare books. My father has even published and edited a book on the subject that has become one of the industry's bibles. If I were you, I would come to eBay having decided on a type of collectable you are looking to either collect or make a mint – preferably both.

This is more bigger-picture stuff and I can't tell you what to collect. I can hint at a few things of course but just be aware that it is better to be knowledgeable about one area – a master of something, rather than a Jack of all trades.

Let's say you have done the local car-boot fairs for few a weeks, inspired by my chapter on collecting rare books: then hold back your good items until you have sold at least two or three lower-value books.

Make sure these first few listings have really low minimum bids/no reserves to get things really cooking. Once the sale is over, ship these off immediately, without waiting for payment. More buyers will take a punt with you once you have a few good feedback comments to your name in the Meet The Seller description box.

WHAT NOT TO SELL

My focus is collectables rather than the mountain of other types of goods that get traded at auction, car boots and on eBay. If you want to keep a clean bill of health and indeed, avoid prosecution, you need to apply some common sense to deciding what you can and cannot offer for sale.

eBay has a clear view on prohibited items such as travel tickets, pets, forged items (including celebrity autographs), police uniforms, bulk email lists and firearms. There is also a sea of unclear items that include some types of collectable – you will need to check their guidance on artefacts and vintage 'alcohol' for example. Booze isn't allowed, but unopened items where the value is in the container are. Do check first. eBay has a list of prohibited and restricted items – best read it.

MONEY MATTERS

Some folks don't realise that you have to pay a little something to keep the eBay machine working. You don't see much advertising on the site itself, and eBay doesn't charge buyers. The funding comes from the sellers! It can add up if you pull out all the stops, so please ensure you are aware of the basic types of fees you might have to pay. In brief these are:

- An Insertion Fee – similar to a traditional auction house's lottage. It can range from a few pennies to a couple of quid depending on your reserve or starting price. If your starting or reserve price is between 1 and 9p you pay 15p as an insertion fee. At the upper end, £100 or more attracts a fee of £2.

- A Reserve Fee – this is an additional fee which you pay to set a reserve on your item. This is refunded if your item sells. For example, if your reserve price is set at £50-4,999.99, you will pay 2% of the reserve price if the item fails to sell.

- Final Value Fee – this is very similar to the commission that a traditional auction house charges except for the fact that it is on a three-level set up. In other words there are three different thresholds each with their own percentage cut.

  For example, a final auction 'hammer' price of £600 and above attracts a fixed commission of 5.25% of the first £29.99 (£1.57), and then 3.25% of the initial £30-599.99 (that's £18.53), and then, lastly, 1.75% of the remaining closing value balance. This clearly compares rather favourably to the auction house commission.

- Optional Extras and Fees – you can pay extra cash to give your listing the kind of profile that… well, money can buy. While you are placing your item up for sale, you will be offered all manner of extra features designed specifically to help your gem sparkle among everything else. You pay for it. For example, you can pay £49.95 for a special home-page featured listing. This gets your item onto the eBay home page! You'll need to have achieved a feedback score of at least 10 in order to use this listing upgrade.

READY TO LIST YOUR ITEM FOR SALE

Get your item out in front of you and make sure you have a digital camera to hand. Most buyers will be expecting to see an image or two beside your item's description. Hopefully you will own a digital camera. You will at least know somebody who can lend one to you, that's for certain. They are so cheap these days – under £100 for something absolutely superb. eBay is a good place to find cheap digital cameras, new and used. Many mobiles now also have a 1 (or more) megapixel camera built in. That would be fine, and you just send them to your computer by Bluetooth or email.

I would set up a clean white sheet in your front room to use as a background and use blue coloured bulbs in your main light. For smaller items, a task lamp with a blue bulb is fine. Lighting the item sympathetically and avoiding harsh hotspots and shadows is the goal here.

It is important to keep the size to a minimum to allow the picture to load quickly when a potential bidder visits your auction item page. You don't want an unacceptable lull at this point – don't keep them waiting – they will simply click off the page and return to the other listings to continue their search.

Take three or four good, clear pictures. Import them into your computer. If you have a photo package that allows you to tidy up the image – then use it. We are talking about adjusting contrast, cleaning up the background and the like. You should also crop the picture to make the item the key focus of the frame where possible. Almost all word processing packages offer some form of picture and photo editing. iPhoto on the Mac is standard and many people have packages like Photoshop which make all this stuff a doddle, particularly with the 'save for web' tool.

Setting the image resolution to 72 dpi (dots per inch) is the standard way. Keep the finished image to under 450 pixels in width – around 4 inches square. Make sure you save the finished images as JPEG files. I would also check the size of the file after you have saved it. 40–80kb is quick to load these days.

JAMIE'S TOP TIP

When preparing your item's photographs, avoid the temptation to remove blemishes, scratches and cracks or nicks. Despite being simple to do, you will find that the buyers will not be happy if they discover you've doctored the photo. Bad feedback. Refunds. Getting kicked of eBay? Don't do it!

THE SELL YOUR ITEM FORM

This is where you set your item up and get to make all the key decisions. It is incredibly intuitive to use and is, quite simply, self-explanatory. Some of it is just box ticking and you should have already thought about how you are going to pitch your sale. Within this area you will do all the key things that include:

- Selecting the category your item will be listed under.
- Describing your item.
- Setting a reserve.
- Adding a picture to the gallery.
- Setting your minimum bid – many canny sellers set ultra-low ones but also protect themselves with a reserve price (or the lowest price they will accept at auction).
- Deciding how long the auction is.
- And deciding on whether you want to offer the Buy It Now option.

In this area you also set the terms and conditions of your sale: who pays for postage, what your payment methods are. It is here that you can choose to boost the listing's profile with highlights, home-page features and using bold and other options – at a price!

ADVICE FOR SELLING YOUR ITEM

Selecting the right category is important. Getting your title right is essential. The last time I looked, there were over 1700 categories. Which one do you choose to sell your item in? Think about what you do when you buy from eBay. Follow these useful insider tips too:

- Do your own searches on eBay to find out what categories are being used on similar items to yours.
- Don't worry too much about getting the category spot on. If you are starting out, it doesn't actually matter too much as most users search for collectables by entering key words. Some will also search for words in both titles and descriptions (it is easy to do both).
- Choosing an appropriate and compelling title is far, far more important as searches are based on this key information.

- Include your item's name, the artist, or even the designer
  if appropriate.
- Avoid the common mistake of using words such as 'amazing' or
  'look'. Potential bidders simply don't search for key words like these.
- You have just 45 characters to pitch your wares! Clearly declare
  what the item is e.g. 'Corgi Aston Martin'. If you know it is the
  rare vintage model from the 1960s, then say 'Original Corgi
  Aston Martin'.

What else is important? Well, I can tell you that the vintage model came in two colours and that affects values. It is also important to many collectors that it is mint and boxed. Again, state this. An example therefore would be 'Original Corgi Silver Aston Martin Mint/Boxed'. Other magic words which I can share with you include Rare, Vintage and Collectable. I would advise you to get familiar with the various abbreviations that seasoned users take advantage of: MOC is known as 'Mint on Card' whist MIB is common jargon for 'Mint in Box'. That last abbreviation will save you around a fifth of your allocated characters.

GET YOUR ITEM'S DESCRIPTION RIGHT

You can now pop the item in front of you and set about describing it in a compelling, dynamic, succinct and truthful manner. All these words are important. Also:

- I would use the HTML text editor that eBay provides to spice up
  the layout, but always aim to keep the main points to the point.
- If we are using the Corgi toy as the example, I would use bullet
  points to highlight the positives: the condition, the fact it is in a tidy
  box, I would suggest the 'grade' of the box, too. Underline the fact

that it is a classic collectable and not that many in this condition can
be found.

- If you value future custom and positive feedback, include the
  negatives if there are any to declare. This would include details that
  might not be apparent in the photos.

- Some sellers include popular search words in their descriptions to
  boost the number of visitors – despite being accidental visitors. This
  is known as 'keyword spamming' and is against the eBay rules.

- Mention your basic terms and conditions here including any
  postage details and payment methods you accept. I would also
  drop in the dimensions to avoid confusion down the line. Though
  it is not required, almost all sellers will factor this info into their
  item's description.

- Be polite – wish the potential bidder 'Good Luck' or 'Happy
  Bidding'. I have seen some absolutely awful item descriptions that
  are downright hostile! They rattle on about how many times they
  have been 'shafted' and how they are 'not going to let it happen
  this time around'. I have also seen the more familiar negative
  approach, which just leaves a nasty impression – 'Don't bid unless
  you mean it' etc.

- If you are uncertain about the type of wording to use for your item
  description and indeed, the starting price or minimum bid you
  might wish to use, then I would browse around and search for
  similar or identical items to see how the competition is playing it.
  Have they sold the items? Were there plenty of bids made? What
  was the final price paid?

- Don't forget to spell check.

> **JAMIE'S TOP TIP**
>
> Avoid using visitor counters. I find that basic psychology comes into play. When users are browsing and come across your item – if it has been viewed by loads of people, but has attracted few, if any, bids (quite likely in the early stages of many auctions), then it will appear as if there is somehow something wrong with your item or worse, your reputation. Stack the odds in your favour, and unless you have a clear reason for monitoring visitor numbers, keep the counter off your auction item page.

IT'S ALL ABOUT TIMING

What do you do when you have to decide on the duration of the auction? It is actually just a matter of clicking a box – but there is much more to it in terms of strategy. Seasoned eBay sellers (and buyers) are aware of the different time zones, the seasons, fashions and trends. It should become your mission to know this information and much of this comes with experience. However, let me help shorten the steep learning curve and give you a shortcut here:

- You only have five choices for the length of your auctions – one, three, five, seven, and ten days. Which is the best for you do you think?
- I would suggest five- or seven-day auctions. Ten removes the sense of urgency and three could mean you miss out on folks searching and noticing your item. Three is good for items which are ultra desirable to collectors as it creates a perceived 'limited availability' mindset. I have found that if you make something rare and then less attainable, you create a natural demand. Think what some toy

manufacturers have been rumoured to have done with brand new items in the run-up to Christmas!

- If you are selling in the UK only (my advice to start out with), then don't end your auction at 4am on a Tuesday morning, as most bidding still takes place in the last hour. Don't scupper your chances of making a mint by selling while we are all asleep.
- With collectables, I find that most potential bidders are online in the evening, at lunchtimes and at weekends – Sunday, or better still, Saturday evening at 8pm or 9pm is probably your optimum end time for the auction.
- There is a little catch here though: you can't select your auction end time! The eBay system makes it tough to actually select the ending time you want. The time of day that you begin the auction is the time of day that it ends. So if you begin at 1am, your auction will end at 1am. Not great for reasons I have described above.

GO!

Hopefully you have written a great description for your own collectable. It is then a simple process to check your page by previewing it. Once you are happy, you simply click on the 'Submit My Listing' button and the auction begins. You might not see it straight away, but it should be up within a few minutes. If you do spot some errors you are able to go back in and amend them. Remember, if you are a new seller, you need to be on hand from time to time to answer any questions potential bidders may have. They will email you and you can choose to display the answer to that question in front of the other users too. Five questions and answers can be displayed like this, which acts as a FAQ and saves everybody time.

THE END OF YOUR AUCTION

As the seller, you have clear obligations to the successful bidder. I would suggest you follow these basic steps to ensure you keep your customers happy and keep that all-important feedback score sparkling.

- *Keep all records*: Keep both paper and emails copies of all your transactions. Set up a specific file for these. The main page you want to keep is the auction item page as it was at the close of your sale. This has all the key details for your records. Also keep all the correspondence between you and your buyer and any payment details and bank statements. All these help keep the taxman or your accountant in the loop and may be useful if you have a dispute with the buyer down the line.
- *Respond asap*: Try and get in touch with your successful buyer as soon as you can. You must do this within three days. Make sure you are not away on holiday or without Internet access while this is happening.
- *Shipping*: Get the item posted off as soon as payment has been received (often immediately with PayPal) or the cheque has cleared. I have sent off the items before payment is received to build trust and future business opportunities. Make sure you have packed it well. You can add a modest fee of a quid or so upfront in the item's description to cover packing materials. Keep it reasonable and don't try to profit from packing as it will be spotted.
- *Keep in contact*: Stay in touch with your buyer through the process. Send a congratulatory email at the start – and keep this polite and friendly communication going. Thank them for their custom – ask if there is anything else you can do to help. Also, let them know when they are likely to receive the item.

FEEDBACK MATTERS

eBay uses a unique community-based ratings system that means buyers and sellers have a compelling motive to deal fairly with everybody. I have explained the feedback system in more detail in the chapter about using eBay to buy, but there are plenty of extra points which apply particulary to the seller. My experience has been that most sellers will put that extra effort in to make the deal feel good because it can mean you get great, above average feedback left for all to see and you are likely to get repeat sales from satisfied buyers.

I have even found, as a buyer, that some sellers will dispatch the items before payment has been received. This is about trust and it is a great thing to encounter in cyberspace with a complete stranger.

I would follow that model and be the perfect seller. With lower-value items, just send them out immediately. You are taking a small chance but you are going to make a really lasting impression. It's the law of reciprocity at play and that is a powerful thing when it comes to trading and business in general.

Negative feedback is unlikely to be given unless you are clearly and deliberately ripping buyers off. In general, psychology is at work and most buyers are reluctant to give negative feedback, even when they think they are in the right, because you might be likely to leave negative feedback in return – thereby scuppering their chances of a clean bill of health.

JAMIE'S TOP TIP

As soon as the deal is complete I make it a rule to enter positive feedback for my customer. I back that up with an email saying that I have done this. This, of course, usually means they will remember to do the same for you.

12

BECOME A
DEALER

WE HAVE LOOKED at eBay and other great outlets, but what about having a crack at tapping into your very own inner Lovejoy? It is not as crazy as it first seems. Firstly, if you are selling on eBay, you are effectively trading like many other top antiques and collectables dealers. What's now stopping you from taking the title for yourself? You can always give it a whirl and as I said earlier, it might just change your life.

We are mainly talking about having a go at selling (or 'stalling out') at antiques and collectables fairs here. Many professional antiques and collectables dealers fell into the job. Indeed, I started out by taking a stall at a well-known London collectables market for a one-off sale of some of the pieces I had bought cheaply over a few months car booting. I ended up staying there.

For many experienced dealers, particularly those who 'stand' (have a stall) at some of the regular antique fairs, it is fairly hard graft. Many will sleep in their cars or vans overnight as margins can be small and savings need to be made to make their business work.

But then again, by becoming a dealer you often get the chance to sell directly to the most eager buyers – and the ones who often pay top whack – the collectors. You also get to be your own boss. Don't underestimate the joy of effectively being in command of your own destiny. Sure, you are going to be open to all sorts of uncertainties, but you trade that for your freedom. In my old unit there were some incredible people who had had remarkable former lives, from pop stars to dancers. There's also a sense of camaraderie between dealers, especially if you have a permanent space in a centre or market. It sometimes feels like your own little family.

So, you have got some stock, you've sorted out your tax position, you have got the bull by the horns and you are willing to become a dealer for a day. I am briefly going to introduce you to a few different places to consider. Many of the points from earlier chapters regarding preparation and selling also apply here.

ANTIQUE FAIRS

These are the nuts and bolts of the business. If you haven't been to an antiques fair, the time to go is *before* you venture forth. They are an eclectic mix of the best elements of car-boot fairs (multiple stallholders, one- or two-day events, often fast moving and indoor/outdoor) and antique shops (sellers are mostly professional dealers, and well organised and have reputations to maintain).

How to Find

Decide which type of fair is best suited to your collectables. Antiques fairs often cover this category but you must check beforehand. You can find most of what you need to know in the industry bible, a quarterly publication called *The Antiques Trade Calendar*. It costs £9 and can be ordered by calling 020 8922 8257.

Another superb resource is the Fairs Calendar posted on the Antiques

News website. It is fairly substantial, too. Go to www.antiquesnews.co.uk to check it out.

Preparation

You need to prepare properly, especially if it is your first event. Take pens and paper to note down sales. A receipt book is essential so is a calculator. I would also pack more carefully than you would do for a car boot as you may well be travelling further this time. Be selective in what items you choose to bring with you. It isn't a matter of piling it high; catching the eye of your fellow dealers and collectors is what counts.

You may well be provided with a table in a hard standing/indoor event. Check first with the organisers before lugging your pasting tables along with you.

JAMIE'S TOP TIP

If you follow my advice and decide to check out a few good fairs first as a buyer, why not make it pay by taking along a few choice items you have stockpiled and flog them direct to the stallholders who are interested.

ON THE DAY

Many dealers will overnight at or near the venue. If you do leave your vehicle, then cover any boxes, or better still, empty your vehicle. That is of course a touch problematic, hence the hotel known as your car. A compromise might be to stay in a bed and breakfast and pack the most valuable items separately in a plastic box to remove before you leave the vehicle.

When you get to the venue, you will find presentation counts. Make sure you have roughly planned your layout. With experience, you will know what goes where. Seasoned sellers invest in flexible shelving, cabinets and trolleys. Wait to see if it is for you before jumping in with such outlays. Other than that, you should be set to go.

Somebody might come around during the day to collect the rent. It can range from £10 right up to £75 or more for a single day event. As with all transactions, keep your receipts.

A word on prices. You should know beforehand what you need to ask for (or actually get) in order to 'make' on any given item. Don't leave it to the day of the fair – you may well get lost in the haze of it all.

> **JAMIE'S TOP TIP**
>
> When setting up your space, things can be quite frantic. The doors open at a fixed time, ready or not! Why not spread some goodwill and offer to get your adjacent neighbours some refreshments? The law of reciprocity works marvels. When you come to ask them to watch your stall for a while (while you go off and do mini deals or take loo breaks), you will find them far more co-operative. Offer to do the same for them at the very start of the day and you are onto a winner.

Swapmeets, Collectors Fairs, Specialist Fairs

Before we end, don't forget that there aren't just antiques fairs: there are dedicated fairs for time periods, design eras (e.g. Art Deco) and of course swapmeets. I've been to a fair few – from honeypot events to the huge memorabilia fairs. There you can sell directly to an often captive audience and you know that anything you bring may appeal to at least one buyer. You are also more likely to get close to, if not what you actually want, in terms of money.

JAMIE'S
FAVOURITE
COLLECTABLES

Lights, Camera… Action! Sharing my passion while presenting an episode of
Everything Must Go! for ITV1 © The Kent Messenger

INTRODUCTION

WELCOME TO THE third part of my book! Despite the emphasis being how to make money, the very best way to make a mint is to do so while doing something you actually enjoy. I used to spend time visiting collectors' homes in the late 1990s when recording *Collectors' Lot* for Channel 4. Many of these folks had literally let the collection take over their lives, and in some cases it had become more important to them than allowing for enough space to live a decent life. If you are going to collect as well as make a mint then don't let it overrun your life and the lives of those around you.

I don't want to tell you all about buying and selling collectables to just leave you scratching your head asking 'Er… that's great, but what should I now buy and sell?' So I have chosen to tell you about my favourite Top 20 collectables. These aren't necessarily the top best-performing areas, but more my personal favourites. Sure, most areas have experienced some growth over the last few years, but it is important to be aware of the huge variety of goodies out there to keep your eyes on. Information is power – if you know that a Magic Roundabout playset is worth well over £500 in a box, in good shape, you are certain to snap it up at a car-boot fair when you come across it. You can then go to an auction house and make a mint. Follow my advice in the previous section about auctions, and sell it for its market value, or more...

Get familiar with the huge array of collectables out there. Knowing the history of trends sharpens the eye. Make notes of areas that interest you, or perhaps you have identified some items that you already have stashed away up in the attic? I hope the following pages will give you a sense of the market, get you fired up and get you out there. Remember that prices for collectables in particular depend on condition and often the condition of the packaging. All figures mentioned should be treated as a rough guide.

14

AUTOGRAPHS

My two signed Jacko albums © Jamie Breese

I had to begin this section of the book with one of my absolute top collectables. Without a doubt, this area has enormous colour, but is also one of the subjects that happens to have undergone truly enormous growth since the mid–1990s. We are talking huge price leaps and lots more collectors. Indeed, I would like to offer to you one of my best-kept secrets. I have come to the conclusion that the future is going to be dominated by memorabilia, of which, a good part is connected to autographs.

You are probably curious about the pictures. All the business about Michael Jackson in the last few years reminded me of some unusual Jacko memorabilia that I had stashed away years ago. I was lucky enough to receive not one, but two copies of the Bad album signed personally for me in the 1980s. However, what is truly golden about these gems is the fact that one contains Jackson's cat's pee all over the cover. He apparently left the first copy on the floor and when his back was turned, his cat relieved himself all over it. He kindly provided a further copy with the inscription 'To James Breese — Sorry about the cat!'

Philip, Jamie & Fern © Jamie Breese

The two album covers created a bit of a stir – and a few familiar uncontrollable giggles from Fern – when I took them on to ITV1's *This Morning*. From this strange occurrence one can lift two important nuggets of info to pass on to the novice autograph collector. Firstly, try and avoid getting items personally dedicated to you and secondly, it is far better to have his cat's pee, than not, as it forms an interesting story which may add some value for a potential buyer in the future.

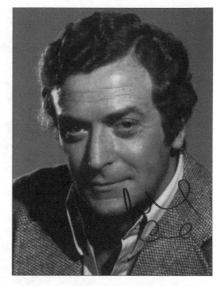

This studio photograph with signature is worth £275 © Image Courtesy of Fraser's Autographs

Philography is big business today and there are even a number of high-street stores and important auctions dedicated to signed artefacts: from simple pages from autograph books to the more colourful signed personal memorabilia such as drum kits and underwear. The market is prone to the laws of supply and demand, fashion and the unexpected, as many items relate directly to the present fame of an individual which can, as we all know, go down as well as up.

ACQUIRING AUTOGRAPHS

If you are interested in starting a collection, then you can consider a whole variety of ways of acquiring that all-important scribble. As mentioned, there's a number of high-street stores these days which usually offer guarantees and belong to professional associations. They sell

A signed Shirley Eaton photo appeals to both autograph and Bond fans

© Image Courtesy of Fraser's Autographs

items in quality frames and you have a point of reference if you are unsatisfied. One of the best examples is www.famousretail.com.

Most auction houses sell autographed items. Occasionally bidding can go through the roof on top lots. Auction houses are less likely to risk their reputation by selling unchecked items. The Internet can be a fertile and cheap hunting ground, but can also be risky as there is a less easy route to travel if you have a grievance. Antiques and ephemera fairs are occurring all the time and can be good places to pick up some more esoteric examples. It's worth remembering that dealers will be less likely to spoil their reputation by passing off unchecked items.

TOP AUTOGRAPH TIPS

In my opinion, the best and cheapest avenue for acquiring autographs is DIY. This is a really good way to make a mint. Think about this. If you just get two celeb autographs (in the over £75 category, like Robbie Williams) a week and sell them each week on eBay, then you are looking at an extra £600 per month. You should find out where the celebs favourite hot spots currently are, such as clubs and bars, book signings, back-stage and at stage doors, and even memorabilia fairs (where they sometimes charge a small fee), conventions and parties. Do some Internet research on the latest 'in' places and make sure you are there, or at least outside with the paps!

Also, writing to celebrities, even Hollywood stars, often yields a signed photograph. Artists' managers and agents will usually handle or forward mail to the talent or their representatives. Many people forget this vital fact. One afternoon a week letter writing and one evening trading on eBay and the cash could really start to add up.

An autographed photo of Fred and Ginger

© Image Courtesy Fraser's Autographs

Though there are plenty of exceptions to the rule, I have a 13-point list of the more general points to remember:

1. An autograph on a scrap of paper or within an autograph book is traditionally worth less than one appearing on a hand-written letter, poster or photograph. However, if that

scrap of paper is something interesting, say the back of an early Beatles concert handbill, then it's going to be worth a bit more.

2. If you've got an autograph book, then get one signature per page, unless it's a band. Never get the reverse of that page signed by the next person!

3. Try and ask for a signature in ink. This is considered better and more reliable in the long run than pencil.

4. Also remember, some celebrities are known for signing in a certain colour. For example, collectable author Philip Pullman is better known for signing in blue ink than black.

5. Putting my Jacko albums to one side for a moment, in general, a personal inscription to a fan along with a signature is usually worth less than a good, clear signature on its own. This is usually because of the way it affects the later sale of the item. Collectors prefer just a signature – perhaps they like to imagine it as having been signed to them! They often display them in their own home. Again, this would be different if Marilyn Monroe signed a card or photo for say, Frank Sinatra. There's an almost historical significance there.

6. In many cases, it is handwritten letters, instruments or items of personal clothing – signed – that command the really big figures. This crosses over into the general memorabilia market, but is worth noting.

Dickens' signature is so sought-after that even a tiny slip of paper can fetch over £1,500 © Image Courtesy of Fraser's Autographs

7. The bigger the signed photograph, the better. The standard signed print is 10 x 8 inches and many of these are pre-signed by pop or movie stars in bulk and then distributed upon request by their representatives. Beware of what are known as facsimile autographs – those printed onto photographs. These are worth very little.

8. Quite often, asking for a simple drawing, perhaps a caricature, together with a signature is always interesting when it comes to a collector. Alfred Hitchcock would often add his trademark line drawing of his profile and it adds value – around £400 in total at auction.

9. If you are asking a famous author to sign, consider asking him or her to both sign and date if the new book has just been released that week; or ask them to add a catchy line from the story. If you are asking a movie star, then think about their best role: Sir Ian McKellan's photograph is worth more if it is signed with his real name and 'Gandalf' in brackets.

10. Condition and authenticity is of the utmost importance. Ask questions before buying an autographed item. If you are the DIY type, then – perhaps at a controlled book signing – ask permission to take a photograph of the item being signed.

11. If asking for an autograph in person, always be courteous and accept refusals gracefully. There is no reason whatsoever why a personality should provide their signature for you, a stranger, though many professionals will see it as flattering, part of the job and good PR.

12. Look after your precious acquisitions. Direct sunlight and damp should be avoided when storing or displaying them.

13. If you think you have a genuinely valuable autograph, then you will find that many experts, dealers and collectors use authentic scanned signatures for close comparison. There are plenty of fakes out there, or items which crossover into a grey area such as those created by the autopen and signatures made on behalf of a personality. Best to research your chosen area carefully and watch prices at auctions and on the web.

By the way, my Jacko albums are probably worth between £200 and £300, when at one point in the late 1980s they could've fetched up to £800. I gave them away for a special charity auction on one of our episodes of *Everything Must Go!* We were raising money for a permanent hospital bed for a girl called Poppy who had a brain tumour. I think some generous lady paid around £250 in the end. Sometimes you need to pass on your good fortune to somebody else who could really benefit.

GREAT SIGNATURES
Greta Garbo
Garbo hardly ever signed anything and is thought to be the rarest screen icon at £3,000+ for a signed photo. This demonstrates the supply and demand nature of the market. I'm told that another silver screen legend, Joan Crawford, spent 8 years signing all day long.

David Beckham
For comparison, one of the most popular living sports celebrities, David Beckham, is a very generous signer. He rarely says 'no', especially if a charity is involved. It is relatively easy to come by good, clear signatures on photos, shirts and footballs. Today, his autograph on a photo, if nicely framed, can make around £90–160. However, Christie's once sold a pair of Beck's boots for £13,800 on an estimate of around £1,000!

William Shakespeare
Possibly the rarest signature of all would be that of William Shakespeare.

AUTOGRAPHS

There are six known, authenticated signatures on documents including his will. Some people have suggested amounts in the early millions for any signed document if one came up for sale. A genuine manuscript, if one surfaced would be truly priceless – certainly something to give Picasso a run for his money. £50 million+ anyone?

Other collectable authors include Charles Dickens: a signed photograph would be of enormous interest to a collector and could easily make over £1,000 if genuine. John Ronald Reuel Tolkien's autograph is very hard to find and would be worth several thousand pounds.

The Beatles

In the past few years the asking price for authentic signatures of the Fab Four have risen dramatically. This could be linked to the untimely death of the great and gentle George Harrison in 2001.

A clean set of signatures in blue ink that fetched £2,031 at a Christie's auction in May 2003

© Image Courtesy of Christie's Images Ltd. 2006

131

Around 70% of autographs from after 1963 were signed on behalf of the band by two assistants. Before that date, the band would usually do the handiwork. There is a sliding scale for signed Beatles' items which goes from separate autographs right up to signed album covers which all fetch many thousands, though *Sgt Pepper's Lonely Hearts Club Band* is considered the most desirable by many.

Top autograph experts Fraser's valued a signed photo at £4,950 in 1997. In 2005 they put it at £17,500. For John Lennon, the figures are £675 and £3,950.

Other popular autographs include Sir Sean Connery: considered the best Bond and a hard signature to acquire. An autographed shot is worth around £200 at present; Rudolph Valentino: he usually signed his full name, but for friends he would use the names 'Rudy' or 'Rudolfo', along with an inscription. He usually added the date to any autograph, too. £1,000+; Stan Laurel and Oliver Hardy often make £200–600 for a signed photo postcard; Royalty isn't so hot, but interest remains strong in Diana's signature, which is currently worth thousands of pounds; Robbie Williams makes about £100–150 for a signed 10 x 8 and Elton John is a steady seller with a price tag of around £100–150.

Where to Find out More
- One of the top dealers of signed memorabilia is: www.frasersautographs.com.
- Christie's the auctioneers frequently sell signed pieces: www.christies.com.

15

COLLECTABLE CORGI

© Image Courtesy of L.Tiley/Corgi Classics

I HAD THE honour of hosting and judging the Corgi Ultimate Collector Competition recently, selecting a winner from multiple entries worldwide. I announced the winners at Corgi's 50th birthday bash and even had the opportunity to sit in the 007 cars – the Aston Martin DB5 and Vanquish.

Very few manufacturers can claim to have created so many icons as Corgi. Who could ever forget the Yellow Submarine, the silver 007 Aston Martin DB5 or the Batmobile Corgis? Despite having changed hands more times than I could mention, the Corgi brand name has managed to survive for half a century: an incredible feat as the world of playthings has been transformed by the rise of the video games console and other electronic distractions.

As I am sure you will be aware, there is a substantial demand for the original Corgis of the past – these classics are discussed in this chapter too. There is a whole grading system collectors use to describe their models, with details such as the intactness of the packaging often of paramount importance. You frequently find Corgis at car-boot fairs and on the Web, so pay close attention to the following if you want to make a mint.

HISTORY

Corgi was founded in the mid-1950s and was the product of the Mettoy Company, which had been creating pressed metal toys since the 1930s. Most people don't realise, but the actual name of this legendary brand came from a link, however tenuous, between the Swansea-based factory and the Queen. Her favourite dog is of course... a certain Welsh breed.

When the company went live in 1956, it offered just ten models. The very first was the Ford Consul costing a most affordable 2s 9d. To today's youth, this would seem a touch less exciting than a Bond tie-in, but in the 1950s every boy wanted a car just like father's and it was a hit.

Here's a bit of trivia which indicates how successful a start the firm really did manage: within three months the initial run of 100,000 had sold out and the factory had to produce a further 250,000 examples to meet the huge demand. Corgi actually made 118,519 more models than Ford did cars in six years!

The 1960s proved the boom time for the company with astonishing successes with so many TV and movie tie-ins – possibly the most fondly remembered Corgis and certainly the most collectable. But the dream was not to last with a tragic fire which destroyed the Swansea factory, set production back and of course allowed the competition to step in to soak up the gradually declining demand.

During the 1970s the firm saw more problems as there were fewer children to play with toys, as well

Jamie and Marcel R. van Cleemput – the very first Corgi designer

© Image Courtesy of L.Tiley/Corgi Classics Ltd.

as a recession. Quite a few other factors combined to lead to an overall decline in the market. However, there were plenty of successes along the way starting with the Whizzwheels which appeared in 1970 as an alternative to Hot Wheels, and the first of the *Magic Roundabout* toys. In 1973 another home run was scored when the John Player Special Lotus won *Toy Trader* magazine's Best Selling Die-cast Toy Award and went on to be a big seller for Corgi.

The 1980s saw chief competitor and fellow die-cast legend Dinky go under. Eventually Corgi faced the same but was saved by a management buy-out at the last minute. The focus of production switched to high-quality and even adult orientated collectable models. Corgi rose from the ashes to seize the coveted title of British Toy Company of the Year in 1987, but even that could not prevent a takeover by Mattel at the end of the decade. Mattel sold Corgi in the mid-1990s and Corgi produced licensed models largely based on British sitcoms and dramas. In 1999, Corgi changed hands yet again. It was bought by a firm that is now known as Corgi International Ltd. and has focused on several areas including the nostalgic recreations from cult TV action series of the past as well as *Dr Who* tie-ins and a special 40th Anniversary *Thunderbirds* series.

Corgi has survived many shifts in fashions and playing habits and clearly remains one of the key names in the collectables market. The rise and continued popularity of the die-cast vehicles and playsets from their past, suggests the company has a bright future if it can keep adjusting to the needs of adult and junior purchasers.

GEMS TO LOOK OUT FOR

I think the special Corgi vehicles discussed below truly capture the essence of collecting today. There's a lovely mix of colour, nostalgia, affordability and a well-established system of trading, with terms to describe the condition of both the box and the toy itself.

Some of these toys have been re-released more recently at a price which gives the novice an easy blast-off point and there's certainly a hint of retro with all the pieces I am going to tell you about.

The whole TV and film toy market has created a growing international craze with books on the subjects and now, specialist auctions, shops and swapmeets. It's certainly harder to find pristine (or mint) finds in their boxes, because toys, and especially toy vehicles, are made to be played with! In my experience collectors find it hard to relate to the older, pre-war items so the cult classics I have lined up on the starting grid are mostly from the 1960s.

© Image Courtesy of L.Tiley/Corgi Classics Ltd.

CHITTY CHITTY BANG BANG

- A Corgi that has climbed high on the collector's wish list is the superb *Chitty Chitty Bang Bang*.

- This was released in 1968. There were several real cars produced for the legendary film and, against the odds, all have survived. One was in a museum in the UK and another is available for private hire. All have the 'GEN 11' number plate that was the closest the producers were authorised to get to the word GENIE by the authorities.

Chitty Chitty Bang Bang *makes £300–500 depending on condition*

© Image Courtesy of L.Tiley/Corgi Classics Ltd.

- The box is bright and fun and boldly announces the vehicle inside as the 'most fantasmagorical toy in the history of everything!'
- Corgi made two versions and the total sales nearly made it to the million mark but watch out for condition as these models were delicate and easily damaged.
- Both are desirable, though model number 266, a 1/42nd scale model with pop-out red and yellow striped wings is the most sought-after and worth around £250–325 if in great shape.
- If you find the version with the deep gold trim (pictured), then you are looking at £400–500 or so, mint and boxed.

THE BATMOBILE

This classic comic strip turned TV hero was recently seen again on the silver screen in the hugely successful *Batman Begins* starring Christian Bale as the Caped Crusader. With every new feature film, interest grows in *Batman*-related merchandise, as does the value of original 1960s toys.

The Batmobile can make up to £450 © Image Courtesy of Vectis Auctions Ltd.

- The ultimate toy would be the actual Batmobile itself! Famously based on the experimental looking Ford Futura – with a few special modifications, it proved to be an instant hit. It was a 19-foot beast made for only two passengers and proved to be perfect for the 1960s TV series. There were several copies made of the original for shows and tours.
- The must-have toy car for any Bat fan must be this legendary Batmobile model 267 made by Corgi.
- The toy came with some important extras such as a flame-throwing rear exhaust, a chain slasher and twelve firing rockets. Also included was a badge and secret instructions pack.
- An astonishing 5 million of these toys were made.
- At present, a near-to-mint boxed example with all the bits mentioned included, will set you back £375–450. The condition of box as well as the toy itself is crucial to getting the best price down the line.

THE AVENGERS GIFT SET

Now we can take a quick look at the wonderful world of another 1960s classic show, *The Avengers*. If we backpeddle one year to 1967 we could find the handsome *Avengers* Gift Set.

The Avengers *Gift Set can make up to £500*

© Image Courtesy of Vectis Auctions Ltd.

- A few years back I took one of these Corgi creations on to *GMTV* when it was going up for sale at Christie's of South Kensington, London.

- It's a delicate little set containing Emma Peel's White Lotus and Steed's unforgettable Bentley. The box itself is a classic of groovy graphic design and really epitomises both the show and the Swinging Sixties.
- If you have a complete, mint and boxed set with all three plastic brollies and the hard-to-find model 'club slip', (a piece of paper about the Corgi Membership Club), you could be around £350–450 better off.

THE MONKEEMOBILE

The *Monkees* TV show first appeared in 1966 and lasted for 58 episodes. The series charted the scrapes encountered by the Beatles-esque quartet who tied in their country-folk-rock music to each episode.

The Monkeemobile © Image Courtesy of Corgi Classics Ltd.

- The real Monkeemobile was a supercharged and heavily customised Pontiac. Only two were made. Both are still in full working order.

- Corgi produced various models but it is the slightly larger Monkeemobile (Model No. 277) that is the one to track down. This contained all the Monkees, has a yellow interior and was packaged in a window box. Today a mint and boxed example will make about £250.
- Corgi also made the Junior Husky Model (No.1004) which is currently worth up to £200 in mint condition.
- Look out also for the Airfix models, too, which were produced as a kit in 1967 and can command £120, unbuilt in a box. The friction-powered tinplate Monkeemobile made by Aoshin is a rare find and can cost £400.

THE MAGIC ROUNDABOUT GIFT SET

For the avid collector, the Holy Grail must be any of the characters or sets used in the original French animation. The Corgi *Magic Roundabout* playground set is the next best thing, showing a rapid appreciation in value in recent years.

This Magic Roundabout *Playset makes between £400 and £900, depending on condition*

© Image Courtesy of Corgi Classics Ltd.

NODDY

Enid Blyton's famous character has captivated millions of people around the world, not just through her books but through the collectables – many of which started life as toys and are now worth good money – which have been manufactured for almost 50 years.

This Big Ears driven car can fetch a couple of hundred pounds today

© Image Courtesy of Vectis Auctions Ltd.

- Noddy first appeared in 1949 initially in *Mr Tumpy and his Caravan* and then in his own book, *Noddy goes to Toyland*, of the same year.
- The yellow Corgi Noddy car of the late 1960s is very hard to find and is considered politically incorrect today, as it has the controversial Golly character sitting in the boot.
- Big Ears is at the wheel and if sold with the picture box in top shape, it can make £200–300 or more today. One version is sometimes seen with light brown Tubby the bear in the boot instead.

ANNIVERSARY EDITIONS

A wealth of special limited editions were released in 2006 to mark the 50th anniversary of Corgi. They were all featured in a special limited - edition catalogue and came boxed in classy retro packaging. Each one was stamped with a 50th emblem and a numbered certificate.

Great news for collectors on a budget, as this is a simple way to actually own a mint and boxed example of a classic toy! The range included a gold-plated Spitfire and the original Ford Consul, examples of which were manufactured in the same way as the 1956 originals with a metal chassis and real windows. The green version (AN01104) came with a book and was a limited edition of 1,000. The gold-plated edition (AN01102) was limited to just 500, so if you come across one of these, snap it up!

The gold-plated Corgi Spitfire, released to celebrate the 50th anniversary of Corgi

© Image Courtesy of Corgi Classics Ltd.

Where to Find out More

- Visit Corgi's website – www.corgi.co.uk.
- Why not visit top auctioneers Vectis – www.vectis.co.uk.

16

CLASSIC AND COLLECTABLE TELEPHONES

THE LAST 15 years have seen an enormous increase in the interest and collectability of the telephones of yesteryear. These often pop up in charity shops and at car-boot fairs and are usually priced very low. Some of the rarer sets can really make a mint if you can track them down.

My own interest stems from my early years as a teenage antiques dealer at Portobello Road and the famous Stables Market in Camden. Even as early as the 1990s, the general public had started to discover the potential value of vintage telephones, largely through media exposure and the revived interest in all things Bakelite. Not so fond memories included what seemed like an endless stream of 'lookers' who would casually saunter on by, pick up the phone and simply talk into it. When asked if interested they would ask how

312 model telephone. £190–200.

© Image Courtesy of The Old Telephone Company Ltd.

much, my eyes would light-up and then the familiar, 'Oh that's great, I've got one in my attic!" would follow.

THE EXPERT'S PERSPECTIVE

…and that's probably why there is so much interest – almost everyone has probably owned an old phone at some point or other. I asked a renowned specialist and writer in the field, Andrew Emerson, why he feels vintage telephones are so popular among collectors and the general public alike.

'There's an element of nostalgia – a flashback to a time when commonplace domestic items were made more solidly than the objects of today. They are also something which you can still appreciate today; they don't take up much room and they make a great conversation piece when friends come around!'

To get a dealer's perspective, I asked Gavin Payne, who is the owner of The Old Telephone Company, based in Essex, what got him started.

'I realised back in the mid-80s that this was something I could do in my retirement, especially given my electronics background. I had an offer of a quantity of Queen Jubilee Telephones. I sunk my savings into buying them. Soon afterwards in 1986, I took them to a fair. The response was very interesting: everyone thought I was mad and I didn't sell a thing! My wife and I tried again at another antiques fair and we had some success – that was it and we didn't look back. I retired from my job in 1990 and set up my business.'

EARLY HISTORY

Though there has been some dispute, it is generally agreed that the device with which Alexander Bell first transmitted speech on 10 March 1876 was the first telephone. There followed a bitter dispute regarding

232 phone with 64d Bell Set. £350 © Image Courtesy of The Old Telephone Company Ltd.

the origin of the invention, eventually settled in the US courts, between Bell and fellow inventor Elisha Gray.

The case, regarding patents, saw the young Bell triumph. He then went on to set up one of America's largest corporations and change the world of communications forever.

Telephones first appeared in Britain when Bell visited Queen Victoria on the Isle of Wight in January 1878 and gave the very first demonstration in this country. Little did he know that telephones made back then would one day be worth so much now. That particular phone now resides in the BT Museum and is a prize exhibit.

IMPORTANT TELEPHONES USED IN BRITAIN

Telephones caught on fairly quickly in Britain. The model names used in the UK often confuse the novice as the firms chose incredibly bland names – usually just 'Type' followed by a number. It is also interesting to note that, for most people, these telephones were only available by renting them from the GPO. It wasn't until the early 1980s, with de-regularisation of the service, that people could actually purchase their own handset.

Featured below are some of the most popular and important examples to look out for. As with many antiques and collectables, it is important to note that the prices, when suggested, are merely a rough estimation, based on what an individual was prepared to pay at that time.

Type 16 Skeleton Phone

© Image Courtesy of The Old Telephone Company Ltd.

EARLY TELEPHONES

One of the earliest and most important early models was the Gower-Bell variety, of which there were several types available. These date from the 1890s and were rather elaborate devices that were fixed to the wall and featured a connecting pipe that was held up to your ear. There was no dial at this stage and your call went straight through to an exchange (the first exchange was developed in 1880). A very fine example could well be worth over £1,000. By their nature, such treasures are particularly hard to stumble upon.

The next important telephone design was the Type 16 or 'Skeleton Phone' made by Swedish manufacturer Ericsson, who are still major players in telephone technology today. It was unveiled in 1898 and had a particularly long period of production. It is a bizarre looking device, which wouldn't look out of place in the set for the film of HG Wells' classic story, *The Time Machine*. Values vary enormously and are, of course, dependent on condition and market demand, though one of these can be picked up for anything between £500 and £1,000.

Collectors look for specific things: a lucky find would be a complete item with the fine black lacquer and gold transfers still intact. A gold and ivory version was made for the Tsar of Russia – that would be a find to phone home about!

The evolution of early telephony continued with the 'Candlestick' variety. The first popular model was the Type 2 telephone made between 1908 and 1929. Its upright design was due to the need to keep the transmitter vertical.

The Type 150 Candlestick telephone was made from Bakelite. Introduced in about 1924, it was almost identical to the US model and proved to be the most popular table telephone in Britain at the time. The main difference was that these phones had dials. A 150 Candlestick with brass No. 1 Microphone (with bellset No. 1) starts from around £780 for a good example. The 150 continued in production up until 1929.

There were so many other telephones made in this period that there could never be enough space to do them justice. However, buyers should be aware that there is a strong and consistent demand for the various wooden–cased wallphones such as the Type 121 or the Type 11.

Type 150 Candlestick phone, £200-250

© Image Courtesy of The Old Telephone Company Ltd.

THE DEVELOPMENT OF PLASTIC TELEPHONES

The arrival of Bakelite, or 'the material of a thousand uses in the early part of the twentieth century eventually found its way into the manufacture of telephones. The series of telephones featured here are particularly robust and their streamlined or 'cleanlined' appearance reflected the general design styles of the period, influenced by the great industrial designers and the Art Deco movement.

- The 162 of 1929 was the first of the so-called 'Pyramid' phones. This was the first telephone to be made almost entirely out of Bakelite.

- The 232s came out in 1934. These were similar to the 162 and continued in production until the mid 1950s. The appearance was much the same, though internally it was slightly different. A standard black model from the 200 series range might set you back anywhere from £200 from a shop such as the Old Telephone Company.

- The 300 series models arrived in 1938 when the GPO version was finally made available to customers and continued its production up until 1959. They featured a one-piece Bakelite housing, whereas the 200s were constructed from many different parts. Variants of these were still being made in India until very recently.

232 phone, approx £250 © Image Courtesy of The Old Telephone Company Ltd.

THE 200 AND 300 SERIES

Red 232 series phone, £1,000

© Image Courtesy of The Old Telephone Company Ltd.

Green 200 series phone, £1,100–1,200

© Image Courtesy of The Old Telephone Company Ltd.

- Models in the 200 and 300 range could often be found with a 'cheesedrawer' which pulls out to reveal a mini address book. The presence of this can marginally increase the value, as does the correct and original bell set.
- The real money however lies in the coloured examples, in particular the 'Pyramids'. These were made in the luxury ivory colour (worth around £500), the upmarket Chinese red, which was also used in fire stations and as an emergency phone in department stores, (around £1,000) and jade green, which was for the discerning individual or some government departments (now worth £1,000–1,200 in fine and original condition).
- The unpopular, and therefore very rare, walnut variety, and gold and silver types, now command a premium.
- There is still the almost mythical Royal blue example, supposedly made for the monarchy, yet to be unearthed. If you are lucky enough to acquire the matching coloured bell sets, you could name your price.

- Rare examples are the quirky aluminium 'explosion-proof' 300 telephones (made to encase sparks and to protect oil refineries and chemical plants), and the clear Lucite plastic examples that were made for special shows or demonstrations.

THE ERICOFON

1949 also saw the first 'all-in-one' telephone from the Ericsson Company in Sweden. Designed by Blomberg, Thames and Lysell, the Ericofon was a sleek, streamlined and functional unit that was lightweight and versatile. The dial was ingeniously mounted on the base. As the Ericofon was not imported into the UK until the early 1980s, it can be tricky to come across one of these unusual pieces, but look out for the brightly coloured versions that were manufactured in the mid 1950s.

THE 700 SERIES

- This series was first introduced in 1959. Designed by Ericsson Telephones and the GPO Engineering Department, this design was a huge step away from the candlestick or brittle Bakelite handsets and proved to be one of the most influential designs of the era.
- Like the Ericofon, it was made from Diakon plastic, which was lighter and could be more colourful than the models of the war years.
- Colours available included ivory and black for the wall phone and lacquer red, topaz yellow and blue for the desk varieties.
- The 700 series continued production until the late 1970s, and despite this, some models in the range are already sought after.
- Lucky finds would include one of the rare coloured examples which were produced as trials or show pieces, such as an ivory and red handset, a clear plastic variety and an experimental tangerine variation. These can be worth upwards of £1,500.

Jamie's Tips and Tricks

1. Reproductions and fakes: Because of the popularity of old telephones, reproductions have been made. There are also copies, particularly of the rare coloured 200s and 300s which are sometimes passed-off as originals: these can prove hard to spot. Look for the original cords; check the bases of coloured examples for over-spray and if in doubt, pass.

2. Care: Bakelite fades severely when left in direct sunlight – rare red Bakelite telephones have been known to turn a salmon pink! Bakelite is not particularly able to deal with extremes of temperature or damp conditions, either. A commercial preparation such as T-Cut is sometimes recommended for cleaning dirty Bakelite. Be aware that it might reduce the gleam over a period of time. A good wax spray can be used for the final polishing-up.

COLLECTING TELEPHONES FOR THE FUTURE

There is no evidence to suggest that the popularity of collecting vintage telephones will let up. My tip for the future, as I've said for many years, is to keep safe your existing mobile phones.

I asked the experts for their tips.

Gavin Payne has one simple bit of advice. 'Anybody with an old phone – please put it in a black plastic bag, somewhere dark and cool and leave it there to appreciate!'

Andrew Emerson is a firm believer in telephones as 'modern antiques'. 'Any of the novelty phones which are not sold in great numbers are worth putting aside now.'

He cites the familiar Direct Line red telephone from the popular insurance commercials. 'These were actually available to buy about eight years ago. In years to come these will prove very hard to come by. The Snoopy character phones are something to look out for and these again can only appreciate in value.'

Mobile Phones

I mentioned a tip for the future. It is of course hard to accurately crystal-ball gaze, we all know that, but there is one thing I have been preaching for the last five years — the future, in terms of hot new electronic collectables, most probably lies with the mobile.

Just think how it now shapes our lives — just like the first mass-made 200 or 300 series phones did in the 1930s, or the radio did during World War Two. I have some hard evidence too: in late 2000, I hosted a game on BBC1's *Generation Game*. I bought on several future collectables and they included a first edition *of Harry Potter and the Philosopher's Stone*. It's doubled in value since!

Another item was the world's very first portable phone model. It first appeared in the USA in 1983 and arrived in Europe in 1986. It was the Dynatech 8600x made by Motorola, valued at £150. In late 2002, I hosted an item on ITV1's *This Morning*. The same phone, again supplied by Motorola, had recently commanded a mind-bending £6,000 on an Internet auction! This, I can't believe, is the going rate quite just yet: more a quirk. But it does indicate a developing excitement.

Think about how many different models there are, what a global market it really is, how we are constantly encouraged to upgrade to the latest model and how few of us keep the things in good shape, boxed, with an eye on their future collectability. In a few years, I strongly suspect that there will be a demand for retro mobiles and it may even be cool, if the technology stills works, to be seen humping around some hefty brick phone – I hear the signal on those little puppies still beats many of today's models!

- Though portable phone technology has been around since the 1940s, it wasn't until 1983 that the first truly portable 'brick' phone arrived. It was the Yuppie's dream! The Dynatec cost a whopping £1,200 back then.

- It is also worth keeping a look out for the early 'transportable' phones that were often fitted into car boots but could be taken walkies (if you had strong enough arms). At the time, the battery life was said to be exceptional.

- Some lucky collectors already own one-off or limited-run luxury handsets produced for special events or publicity deals. There is one diamond encrusted Motorola handset worth £50,000!

- If you are scouring the car boots and charity shops, try and pick up mobiles with their original boxes and instructions – this will add to the desirability in the long run, much as it has done recently with vintage home computers and video consoles.

Where to Find out More

- London's Science Museum (Exhibition Road, South Kensington, London SW7 2DD. Tel: 020 7938 8000) has a specific telecommunications gallery. A smaller display of fine telephones may also be fund at London's Design Museum, Shad Thames, London SE1 2YD. Tel: 0870 833 9955 www.designmuseum.org.

- The Old Telephone Company in Battlesbridge, Essex supplies and buys fine examples of most classic telephones from Britain and elsewhere. Tel: 01245 400 601 or see the website www.theoldtelephone.co.uk.

- Andrew Emerson's book, *Old Telephones,* is published by Shire Publications, costs around £2.75 and is available in most good bookshops.

17

BRITISH COMICS AND ANNUALS

POSSIBLY THE ULTIMATE nostalgia trip for big boys and girls! There can be few material things from our childhood that evoke such feelings as the smell of ink on our favourite comic or annual.

Comics and annuals conjure up memories of holidays, long car journeys, treats at the newsagents and one of the fixed days in an erratic week when you knew your treasured title was due to be delivered.

But who could have imagined at the time that many of the comics and annuals that we cherished momentarily as kids would ever be sought out again, years later by collectors around the world? I am sure you have heard of the excitement that occurs over rare US comics but could the same thing apply to the humble British title?

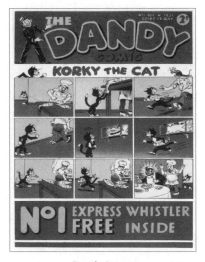

Dandy *Issue 1*

It's a strange thing, but as with serious toy collectors, lost memories appeal to those wanting to recapture their youth and the comic or annual is quite possibly the definitive trip down memory lane.

COMICS

Comic collecting is generally a male activity: currently in the UK, the popular girls' titles don't really achieve comparable prices. It is the home-grown classics aimed at boys, from the *Eagle* to the *Beano*, that create the most excitement.

- As with books, a grading system featuring eight levels has been developed to assist with the description of condition and there are dedicated auctions, traders and fairs where sales take place.
- The World Wide Web has proved to provide a buoyant trading place too.
- The field is generally split into several distinct areas of interest which include the Platinum Age (1897–1932), the Golden Age, the Silver Age and even the Bronze Age!

I thought I would focus here on the classic British titles we all know and love. Of course, the US titles have ignited passions in the past and continue to do so in a much bigger way, financially for sure.

- Possibly the most sought-after comic is *Action Comics* number one from 1938 – this featured the first-ever appearance of Superman.
- Estimates vary, but there are around 75 copies known to exist and it has been priced-up at around the £120,000 mark in good condition!

Back to Blighty, though, and a bit of history here: the first true British comic is now considered to be *Funny Folks*, published way back in 1874, while the first British comic strip hero was Ally Sloper of the unusually titled *Ally Sloper's Half-Holiday*. This appeared from 1884 to 1916.

- It is either the first-ever issue, or the first appearance of a well-known character that grabs the collector's attention.
- Occasionally, comics would come with a free gift as in the case with the first ever *Beezer* from January 1956. This came with a small toy called a 'Whiz-Bang'. The majority were played with or lost, so complete examples are hard to come by and command the best price.

THE BEANO

At the top of most lists of favourite comics would have to be this true survivor of British publishing.

The first ever *Beano* comic appeared way back on the 30 July 1938 and featured a giveaway gift.

- The *Beano* has been published in Scotland by DC Thompson on a regular basis for over 65 years. The Second World War had an unexpected impact on children's staple diet of fun with newsprint restrictions, and it only appeared every other week at this time.

Beano *Issue 1*

© Image Courtesy of DC Thomson Company Ltd.

- Perhaps most famous out of all the characters is Dennis The Menace and his slightly crazy canine companion, Gnasher. Dennis made his grand entrance in 1951 and was a smash hit with readers.

- In terms of today's market, the *Beano* is a heavy hitter. The first annual from 1940 can command over a grand but this is dwarfed by the drive to find copies of the number one comic.
- There are around twelve known surviving copies of the first issue. I first wrote about the price rise years ago when a world record price for a Beano number one comic was achieved by Comic Book Postal Auctions. A single copy sold for £6,800!
- The key is to still have the incredibly rare giveaway – in this case it was the 'Whoopee Sheriff's Mask'. However, this sale was dramatically surpassed a few years ago when the same auctioneers sold a copy for a truly mind-bending £12,100!

ANNUALS

In general, annuals tend to fetch rather less, even if they are the rare first issues. Either way, if you come across an early find for a low figure, always look for the signs which reduce prices, problems such as:

- Messy crayon inscriptions.
- Corner price tag cut out.
- Magic Painting and other puzzles done.
- Uneven, loose spines and dull and tacky covers.

Blue Peter

A few years ago, I had a steep learning curve while preparing for a one-off expert appearance on a *Blue Peter* anniversary show. I gathered loads of info and soon discovered *Blue Peter* to be quite collectable. The first issue appeared way back in 1964 and featured Valerie Singleton (whom I met on the day!) and Christopher Trace on the cover. It's the first three issues that get sold for best prices if complete and in tip-top condition. The first book currently makes between £100 and £180.

Rupert

Rupert annuals are very collectable and the first few issues are valuable. A few years ago, newspapers covered a remarkable sale of a certain *Rupert Bear Annual*. An extremely rare copy of the 1973 *Rupert Bear Annual* made a wholly unexpected £16,500 at auction.

Rupert is fondly regarded by many, many collectors. This particular copy is surrounded with myth now: from my discussions with the auctioneers and collectors, I understood it was one of a handful curiously created with Rupert with a brown face on the cover, but a white one inside. I mentioned this once in my column in the *Sunday Mirror* and received hundreds of requests for valuations on other years. Please note, it is just that year and no other!

This version was rumoured to have been created because of issues between the artist and his publishers. It is worth noting that just three months later, an identical second copy came up for auction but failed to sell.

Beeton and More

One can also unearth all sorts of other lost treasures.

One of the rarest is not quite a children's title and more of a magazine, but the Christmas annuals are the hot ones: the one to hunt down with Holmes-like precision is the 1887 annual published by Ward Lock and Co. This featured the very first Sherlock Holmes story, *A Study in Scarlet*. This is a Holy Grail for the Sherlock Holmes collector. There are 28 known copies today. Where are the others? It cost one shilling back then but today makes up to £100,000 at auction.

The Eagle

Without a doubt, *The Eagle* is one of the most influential annuals of all time.

- The first copy appeared on 14 April 1950.
- It was Colonel Daniel McGregor Dare, tagged the 'Pilot of the Future', who graced the cover of number one and quickly became a national treasure. It was his adventures that were mainly responsible for the great sales the comic and annuals achieved.
- Bizarrely enough, Dan Dare was actually created to be a type of Space Chaplain. This was the objective of the comic's creators – Frank Hampson and the Reverend Marcus Morris.
- Issue one of the comic can command £800–1,000. The annual is slightly easier to come by and it appeared in September 1951. The famous red covers are very delicate and are prone to being scratched so mint copies tend to pull in over £100.

THE CURRENT MARKET

For an insight on the current market, I spoke to Malcolm Phillips at Comic Book Postal Auctions.

'The market is still strong and there are still very large prices that can be paid for items found in absolutely top condition. The market is like many things in collectables – where people are prepared to pay whatever it takes for a top example. *Dandy* comic number one sold for £20,320 where the comic was in fine condition with almost white pages, bright fresh colours and the free gift. The combination of those two things made for a world-record price. By contrast, take a *Dandy* we sold: this had general light wear and tan pages It sold for £6,300 which in itself is a lot of money – but it is still the same number one comic, bearing in mind that only fourteen number ones have only ever come onto the market in the last 20 years.

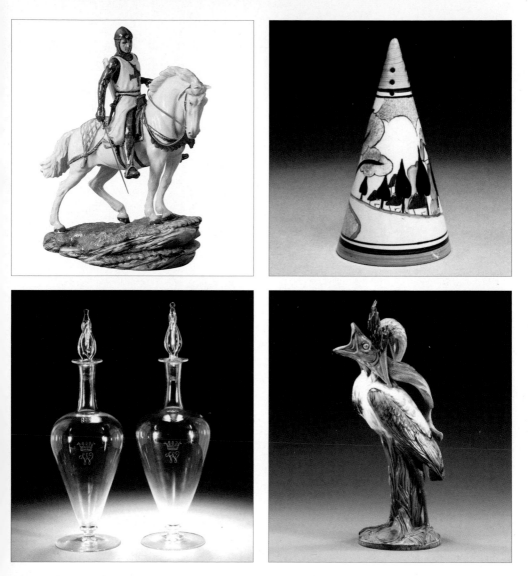

Top right: Royal Doulton's St George figure is exceptionally collectable despite an initial price tag of £10,000. © *Royal Doulton*

Top left: Clarice Cliff is regarded as one of the most influential ceramics artists of the 20th century. This delightful conical sugar sifter from around 1933 had a hammer price of £5,040. © *Sotheby's*

Bottom left: A pair of Whitefriars crested decanters and stoppers from the early James Powell and Sons workshop. Their hammer price with a buyer's premium was £2,760. © *Sotheby's*

Bottom right: Sotheby's hold the world record for Minton Majolica. A heron and pike ewer from circa 1866 would set you back approximately £2,400. © *Sotheby's*

In recent years, the value of toys has risen in leaps and bounds, often outstripping the stock market, banks and building societies. These items from Vectis made a mint for their owners at auction.

Top right: This Lady Penelope car was in mint condition, boxed and one of only 150 produced specially for *Collectables Magazine*. It realized £100.

Top left: A Diamond Planet Robot in exceptionally rare tin plate from Yonezawa in Japan, circa 1960, fetched £7,500.

Bottom left: Sam's car from *Joe 90*, in a well-kept carded picture box sold for £120.

Bottom right: A trade pack of seven *James Bond* Aston Martin DB7s in excellent condition would set you back approximately £190.

© Vectis

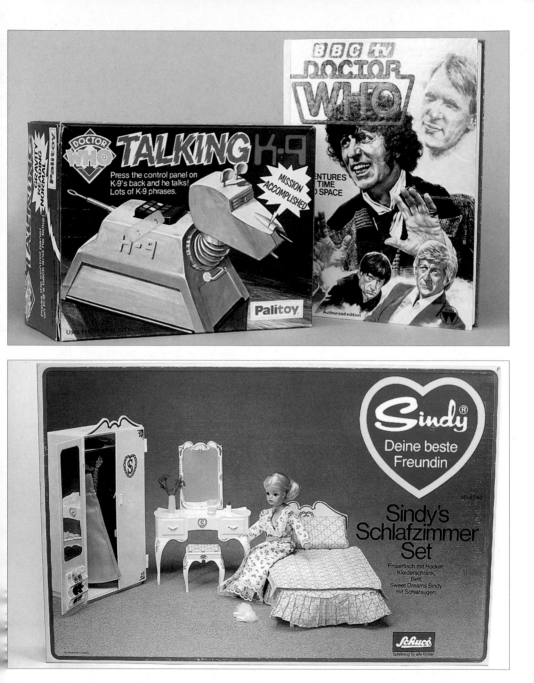

Above: When large collections are put on the market, money can often be made by pairing items together in lots. This talking K9 and *Doctor Who* annual sold for £160.

Right: For a lady in her mid-forties, Sindy still commands a lot of interest! This Schuco Sindy and her Bedroom Set from 1980, including a full-sized doll, is valued at £520.

© Vectis

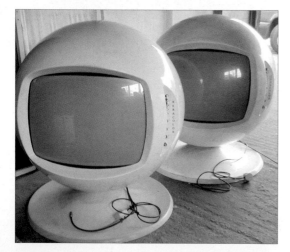

Two very different types of technology with which you can make a mint.

Top left: This Codeg Dalek fetched £440.   © *Vectis*

Top right: A Marx friction drive Dalek, £240.   © *Vectis*

Centre: A well-loved GEC BT1091 television set from 1949, £300–500.

Bottom left: A 1970s icon, the Keracolor TV, made of fiberglass and available in various colours. This white example is valued at £200–400.

© *On The Air Ltd*

'In the British comic world, the most recent big event was the sale of that ultra rare and immaculate copy of the *Dandy*. The *Dandy* first appeared in December 1937 and was bought to us by the same publishers as the *Beano*.'

The sale included the only known example of the metal whistler that was given away with it and a very rare flyer. This went for an incredible £20,350 – a record price for a British comic at auction.

Where to Find out More

- A well-known dealer and auctioneer is Comic Book Postal Auctions. Tel: 020 7424 0007 www.compalcomics.com.
- Why not visit DC Thomson's website www.dcthomson.co.uk?

18

MODERN FIRST EDITION BOOKS

THIS IS ONE of my really hot tips – almost a secret – a specialist area which is relatively easy to get a grip on. And you can start today!

One of the quickest ways to make a mint right now is to go and search the boot fairs, the charity shops and flea markets abroad to uncover these hidden treasures, then sell them on eBay or perhaps one of the specialist rare books sales in the larger auction houses. It really can be that simple if you know the authors and how to identify whether or not a book is a first or not.

I was bought up in a family of bookworms – my mother has been an editor, my father a publisher for years, and my sister has a doctorate in English

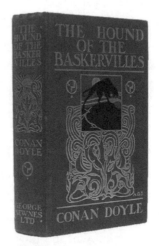

The Hound of the Baskervilles *by Arthur Conan Doyle, 1902 first edition, £3,750*

© Image Courtesy of Adrian Harrington Rare Books

Literature from Oxford. I'm not well-read myself, though I do like to write fiction! It seemed natural to follow in my father's footsteps and start a small collection of fine books several years ago. The problem was, and this has haunted me, the truly huge boom in modern first edition books took place about four or five years ago, so I might have missed the boat. Prices are still rising, as they have been steadily since the 1990s, but it is mind-bending how valuable some of the great books of the last century have now become.

The Day of the Triffids by John Wyndham, first edition

© Image Courtesy of Martin Breese

It's not just the hyper modern titles that have rocketed – and by that, I mean first editions of rare books published in the last ten years or so – but across the board. Read on if you have just a little spare time and want to make a mint.

WHAT IS A FIRST EDITION?

In case you're unfamiliar with the term, a First Edition is a copy of a book from the very first print run. Quite often, with new authors, publishers tend to print very low first print runs – this is usually because the author is largely unknown, and they are reducing their risk by not committing to a vast batch only to find the book facing poor sales and piles heading for the discount book stores. The term Modern First Edition means broadly a title published anywhere from circa 1900 to 1995.

How to Spot One

It is fairly easy to identify a true first edition. As a rule, you should be looking for the first impression of the first edition. Today, most publishers use a numerical 'strike line' on the reverse of the title page, which features (in any order) all the numbers from ten down to zero.

© Kingsmarkham Enterprises Ltd 2001

The right of Ruth Rendell to be identified as the author of this work has been asserted by her in accordance with the Copyright, Designs and Patents Act, 1988.

All rights reserved

1 3 5 7 9 10 8 6 4 2

If the number 1 is missing, then it'll be a second impression (printing) of the first edition state (the same cover with perhaps tiny changes in spelling errors etc.). If 1 and 2 are missing, then it will be the third printing of the first edition and it will rarely be of any value. The big money can lie with the early titles, from top authors in the true first impression/first edition form (or often seen as 1st/1st).

JOHN LONG LIMITED
178-202 Great Portland Street, London, W.1

AN IMPRINT OF THE   HUTCHINSON GROUP

London Melbourne Sydney
Auckland Bombay Toronto
Johannesburg New York

★

First published 1964

Before the 1990s, most publishers simply used the phrase 'First Edition' or 'First Published' followed by a date and no other reference to other editions, dates or impressions. Sometimes you come across famous, rare books, the heart will stop, only to realise what you have in your sweaty palms is a Book Club edition of one sort or another. Again, as a rule, these have no collectable value with one crucial exception: many of Agatha Christie's highly collectable early works were published by the Crime Club. Do not make this mistake with her work – early books in first impression state are worth many thousands if in fine condition.

Condition is Crucial

That brings me to another key factor that occupies the collectable book market: condition.

- If a modern first edition is damaged in any way, the value automatically drops, however scarce the title.
- There is an agreed system for grading books that collectors and dealers use when describing items on the web or in printed catalogues. The best possible state is 'fine in a fine jacket'.
- This means the book is probably unread and 'sparkling' with no nicks or tears, 'foxing' (brown mould-like discolouration on pages), no scratches to the DJ and not price-clipped by the original bookseller or anyone else. The jacket is the dust jacket/dust wrapper, aka the DJ.
- Less desirable features that impact on value include whether the book was once a library copy, or if it has any inscriptions or an owner's bookplate inside.

Bonuses will include an author's signature, though a dedicated signature e.g. 'To Jamie, with Best Wishes' is seen by many as less desirable. A famous quote from the story in the form of an inscription, e.g. 'One Ring to Rule Them All!' from JRR Tolkien, would no doubt prove priceless.

Research First

If I have tempted you to look further into the market, then make sure you gather as much knowledge as possible before spending hard earned cash. Get yourself a collector's guidebook, search the web sites and attend a few book auctions and fairs.

- If you are just starting out, why not get over to a car-boot fair and scan the boxes and boxes of old books.
- When you have gained some knowledge, develop a relationship with a good rare book dealer, as they can often find the lost gems you'll spend a lot of time looking for and they are a vital cog in the book market.
- If you want to make a mint, as opposed to developing a fine personal collection, then best stick to scouring the venues lower down in the buying food chain such as car-boot fairs.

Best Advice

My best piece of advice is, where possible, always try and go for books you want that are in the very best possible condition. If buying from a dealer, it could prove better to pay that extra

The Amber Spyglass *by Philip Pullman,*
first edition, signed and with a fold-out
'Alethiometer' £500

© Jamie Breese

amount for a 'Fine' or 'Very Good' copy as in the long run, they will most likely be the most desirable copies. Try to focus on a few favourite authors to start with and learn how to store your finds correctly.

Lastly, remember, despite the increases in value of many first editions for a good few years now – in fact they've become investment pieces in a way – you must remember that the value of your books can go down as well as up, though depreciation is not very common.

While at car boots, auctions or charity shops, keep your eyes peeled for top authors including, Agatha Christie, Ian Fleming, JRR Tolkien, Ruth Rendell, AA Milne, Graham Greene, Philip Pullman, JK Rowling, Sir Arthur Conan Doyle, PD James, Richmal Crompton and Stephen Spender.

 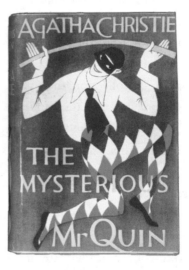

Just William's Luck *by Richmal Crompton,*
first edition

The Mysterious Mr Quin *by Agatha*
Christie, first edition

© Image Courtesy of Martin Breese

© Image Courtesy of Martin Breese

In general, it is the first few novels by a particular author that tend to command the best prices. This is because the first few books by a new author are printed in short runs. In some authors' cases (eg. Tolkien, Brontë), second and third editions can also be quite valuable.

Rarer Titles to Look Out For

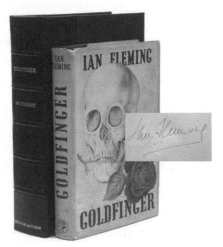

Goldfinger by Ian Fleming,

1959 first edition, £6,500

© Image Courtesy of Adrian Harrington Rare Books

- Conan Doyle's *The Hound of the Baskervilles* (Newnes, 1902). Value: in a DJ, name your price, though £60,000-100,000 would be reasonable!
- Agatha Christie's *The Mysterious Affair at Styles* (John Lane, 1921). Value: in a DJ, name your price.
- Graham Greene's *Rumour at Nightfall* (Heinemann, 1930). Value: Around £12,000.
- Richmal Crompton's *Just William* (Newnes, 1922). Value: in fine DJ is a Holy Grail. Maybe £30,000 or even £40,000.

THE MAGIC POWER OF HARRY POTTER

One cannot go into a discussion about valuable books without a special mention for the bespectacled young wizard. Author JK Rowling's svengali-like powers have caught the imagination of adults and children alike and created a growing and perhaps more dynamic interest in the book-collecting world than any single figure in recent memory.

I once hosted a game on BBC1's *The Generation Game*. Contestants had to guess the value of items I had bought along. One piece was a first edition of *Harry Potter and the Philosopher's Stone*. It was published originally without a dust jacket and cost around £10 in 1997. The audience were dumbstruck when I revealed the value: £10,000!

In November 2006, I contacted the book dealer who had lent me the previous copy and asked to borrow the book again. This time, when I revealed the price tag on a different show, it had increased to a breathtaking £25,000!

There were not many firsts printed as JK was an unknown in 1997. Out of the first print run of 500 copies, 200 were paperbacks for reviewers containing the misprint 'J A Rowling'. Many of the other 300 hardbacks went straight to schools or libraries.

What helped the book early on was the unusually high price paid by a US publisher for the American rights and the talk of a movie option. The staggering success of the film franchise has helped to keep the whole series of books, in the first edition state, at the top of many collectors' wish lists.

The Potter books have benefited too from a series of deluxe editions with gilt-style lettering, no dust jackets and fine bindings. These were printed as limited runs and the first editions, again, can make thousands – especially *The Prisoner of Azkaban*.

Where to Find out More

- I can recommend many book dealers and they would include Adrian Harrington Rare Books, situated at 64A Kensington Church Street, Kensington, London W8 4DB. Tel: 0207 937 1465, www.harringtonbooks.co.uk.
- Why not log on to www.aba.org.uk for a list of other reputable book dealers who operate to a strict code of ethics.
- Specialist sales of books, including modern first editions, are held by the auctioneers Christie's of South Kensington, 85 Old Brompton Road, London SW7 3LD. They can be contacted on 0207 930 6074, or visit the website at www.christies.com.

19

CAMBERWICK GREEN

THE TIMELESS CHILDREN'S series was the brainchild of Gordon Murray. Dreamt up during a visit to his local park, the objective had been to create a 15-minute 'musical spectacular' with the star being the village itself.

Camberwick Green was made at a time in the 1960s when British broadcasting was set in the realms of a black-and-white world; yet Gordon chose to film his masterwork in colour. This was a nifty piece of forward planning as it cost more at the time, but made the show future proof – a fact borne out today with the series still being shown by the BBC from time to time.

Windy Miller

© Image Courtesy of Robert Harrop

The three series, much like *Mr Ben* and *Bagpuss*, have become firm favourites in the UK – there is a whole world of gift items out there, the marketing of which relies heavily on our collective nostalgia for these highly original and often terribly sweet children's TV programmes. Trumptonshire is a slice of a world that never really existed – where all the folk living there were decent and kind and helped one another. This might also account for the huge popularity of the collectables.

The first puppet Gordon created was the postman, even before the scripts had been dreamt up. The actual puppets were created using ping pong balls for heads and polyurethane foam for the body. This basic shape became the standard form from which all

Mr Crockett with his petrol pump is retired, but sells for up to £50. Four years ago he cost around £16 new

© Image Courtesy of Robert Harrop

the characters were created. Stories abound of the entire collection of puppets being chucked onto a bonfire by their maker – no doubt these would have been priceless on the collector's market today.

Camberwick Green was first broadcast in 1966; it was followed by the sister series *Trumpton* in 1967 and finally *Chigley* in 1969. Collectively the shows take place in the world known as Trumptonshire and it is under this banner that Robert Harrop Designs have successfully transferred the colourful screen puppets to the world of collectable resin figurines.

ROBERT HARROP DESIGNS

Robert and Margaret Harrop established their business in 1986. Before forming the firm, Robert had worked for several other companies as a commissioned modeller. They started off in the front room of their cottage and have now moved to larger premises at Coalport House.

Robert Harrop started to produce the figurines in 1998. Eighty-plus different designs of small figures have now been released and several limited and Collectors Club editions together with buildings are also available. Each one is hand-painted, which adds a nice element to the appreciation of each piece. The first figure from 1998, Windy Miller (model Number CG01), is retired, and has doubled in value to around £30 on the secondary market.

HERE IS A BOX

By far and away, the very best investment is a certain musical box. I remember surfing the Web a few years ago and trying to find a gift for my sister. I came across a site offering the musical boxes for £34.95. I decided to buy two, and keep one for myself. For some reason, which I cannot remember, I didn't end up placing the order – and it has cost me dearly. The music box from 2001 was a limited edition of 2,000 and it now sells for £400–600 on the secondary market!

You are unlikely to be able to pick one of these up now as the word is most definitely out. However, you might want to take a punt on 2004's musical town hall

© Image Courtesy of Robert Harrop

clock from the sister series *Trumpton*. It's a limited edition of 2,000 and stands a lofty 14 inches in height. It plays the music that was written by Freddie Phillips and is a working clock, too.

Large as Life

The Large as Life figures are a fairly recent development. I bought one for my mother one Christmas. They stand around ten inches tall and are better for display than some of the larger items. In fact, the name reflects the fact that the original puppets were exactly this size. There are ten characters available, including Windy Miller and Dr Mopp. These are in limited editions of 2,500 each. There are also some very special signed ones around and these are making £250–300 at the moment. As I said to my mother – best keep the boxes with these pieces.

There is also the charming Clown Musical Box that I am told is now quite hard to get your hands on

© Image Courtesy of Robert Harrop

Mini Buildings

Quite a few miniature buildings were released between 2000 and 2003 and some are keenly sought after today. There were two larger models produced prior to these mini buildings: the Fire Station (right) and Colley's Mill. These are far more collectable and the Fire Station has made at least a few hundred on the secondary market.

© Image Courtesy of Robert Harrop

Where to find out more

- The Collectors Club is a good starting point if you are interested in getting serious. They have around 4,500 members worldwide. Robert Harrop now produces Thunderbirds figures and vehicles and Clangers collectables – including a musical box.
- All new members receive a lapel pin, a membership pack, personalised membership certificate and a numbered membership card.
- The club now covers all the Robert Harrop Designs and can be reached on: Tel: 01952 462 721, Email: collectorsclub@robertharrop.com, and by post: Coalport House, Lamledge Lane, Shifnal, Shropshire TF11 8SD.

20

TOY ROBOTS

THE FOCUS OF the news media in recent years has again turned to celestial matters. As various attempts to land probes on Mars take place, I was reminded of how folk in the 1950s imagined the outer reaches of our solar system to be. These images were recorded in the comics, the hugely popular, often fantastically OTT sci-fi films of the 1940s and 50s and the emerging market in space toys.

The launch of Sputnik in 1957 started a global craze for all things space-related and ushered in a Golden Age for the toy robot in particular. Almost all the robots

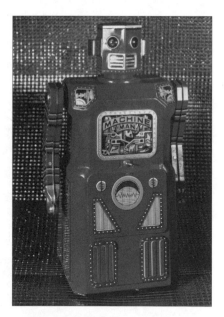

Machine Man sold for £25,000 at the TV Generation sale in July 1999 at Christie's of South Kensington

© Image Courtesy of Christie's Images Ltd., 2006

sold were pitched as being 'from other worlds' and remain a colourful and collectable seam in the very earth-bound world of collectables.

ROBOT HISTORY

The term 'Robot' was supposedly created by the Czech playwright Karel Capek in the early 1920s and came from the word 'robota'. His play was called R.U.R. which stood for *Rossom's Universal Robots*.

Many collectors argue that the very first toy robot was a crude Japanese example called Lilliput. He dates back to the late 1930s but not a lot is known about the company that created him – all experts have had to go by were the mysterious letters K T A. Certainly on the rare occasion that one has come up for sale, it has commanded thousands of pounds. The next documented tin robot emerged in 1949, again in Japan, and featured the exciting name Atomic Robot Man. He is a collector's item today.

The era that saw the big leap in design and production was the decade between 1955 and 1965. So many were made that it is almost impossible to acquire them all, so two broad divisions have been made between the US and Japanese models.

COLLECTING ROBOTS

As with so many antiques and collectables, condition is of the greatest importance when it comes to values. Traders and collectors use a very specific 1 to 10 scale, though it is accepted that almost no vintage toy can be found, boxed, in an 'as new' state. Many of these toys were made with brittle parts or came with easy-to-lose accessories such as ray guns. So, mint, boxed and complete examples carry the highest price tag.

Some of the hard-to-find models would include Mr. Atom, the Electronic Walking Robot, and Robert the Robot, a toy based on a robot

Mr Zerox by Horikawa, £200–300

© Image Courtesy of Vectis Auctions

Dux Astroman Robot – West German,
1950s, £220

© Image Courtesy of Vectis Auctions

from the film *Tober the Great*. Many examples made by manufacturers such as Tomiyama, Nomura, Horikawa Masudaya and Daiya of Japan are worth keeping a look out for too if you seriously want to make a mint.

Any reference to robots would be incomplete without mentioning the legendary 'Gang of Five'. These were five very colourful chaps from the late 1950s who have become ultra rare in recent years. In 1999, I remember one of the five, a red robot imaginatively entitled Machine Man, selling at Christie's of South Kensington, for nearly £25,000!

The demise of the Golden Era of manufacture was signalled by changes in toy regulations: some paint and metal parts were declared harmful and some tin models were withdrawn due to sharp edges. However, plastic production continued until the general popularity of the toy robot waned in the 1970s.

Jamie's Top Tips

If you are lucky enough to uncover a lost toy, do be careful.

1. Certainly don't be tempted to over-wind it if it's clockwork.
2. Keep the box out of direct sunlight and seek an expert's advice.
3. In recent years, collectors and fans have been offered the chance to buy quality reproduction robots with authentic boxes too. This is good news and these themselves might become collectable.
4. On some occasions, I can imagine this has led to confusion between the real McCoy and their modern counterparts. Always check carefully before spending a lot of money.
5. If robots don't fire your imagination or simply appear too expensive to you, why not look at the broader market in space toys. This is truly vast and covers everything from rare Dan Dare tin ray guns to *Star Trek* toy communicators; from pristine packaged *Star Wars* figures to die cast *Space: 1999* vehicles.

ROBBY THE ROBOT

The must iconic of all the great toy robots remains the towering mechanical 'Robby', the legendary automaton from one of the most original sci-fi adventures – *The Forbidden Planet* (1956).

The film caught the public's imagination and was perfectly timed: Sputnik was launched the very next year and there began the worldwide obsession with all things space and Sci-Fi related.

There have been many Robby's made down the years, but the most popular, and today the most collectable, remains the original chap by Nomura Toys of Japan. MGM had strict copyright laws, and it was probably because of this that the toy was called 'Mechanized Robot'.

It's a fabulous original item – I gave one away as a competition prize in the *Daily Mail* years ago. There are black and hard-to-find silver versions. The one to look out for is the large model that stands an impressive 12. 5 inches high and is made of tin. Lights flash, pistons move and antennae swivel as he lumbers along! These toys are difficult to track down in fine condition as sadly acid corrosion from old batteries eats away at the insides and the domed helmet is easily lost.

The best version has to be the original. Apparently, in 1970, the film studio MGM sold the real Robby to the Movie-World Museum in the US but he was partially stripped by light-fingered fans. Robby was later restored and sold to a collector.

Nomura mechanized robot, 33cm, £1,200

© Image Courtesy of Vectis Auctions

The next best thing for the truly dedicated collectors among you will be the full–size, hand-made reproduction Robby with digital features, made by the expert restorer Fred Barton.

Where to Find out More
- Vectis the auctioneers (01642 750616) can be reached at www.vectis.com.
- Full-size Robbys by Fred Barton can be found at www.the-robotman.com.

21

ROCK AND POP
MEMORABILIA

POPULAR MUSIC HAS undergone all sorts of changes in recent years with not only new sounds but also new technology, from the Web to the iPod. One consistent trend, however, has been the continued strength of interest in the colourful world of pop memorabilia.

The Vault Museum at London's Hard Rock Cafe © Image Courtesy of The Hard Rock Cafe

Michael Jackson's lyrics for 'Beat It', £4,200

© Image Courtesy of Sotheby's

A recent sale at London-based auctioneers Christie's proved that the market, certainly at the top end, still looks strong. In serious collecting terms, it is a comparatively new market that saw a big surge of interest in the 1980s.

Many bands of today find an instant collectability, but this is a phenomenon that often can be confused with fandom. The true gauge of greatness is often measured by the desirability of items relating to the act long after they have broken-up, passed their performing peak or even passed away. The Spice Girls were no flash in the pan: they managed to attract both the young fans set on acquiring the right poster or record, and also the more grown-up collector who would shell out thousands for a dress or signed photo. It is questionable now, though, whether an individual today would pay over £40,000 for Gerri's famous Union Jack dress worn at the 1997 Brit Awards. But if you jump ahead thirty years, we may find that girl power will be considered an important era in music and social history, so prices may escalate. As with any collectable, if you are in the game for investment, then it can be an uncertain world.

Certainly the best performers in terms of making a mint have been the best-known acts and I will be looking specifically at some of these acts.

THE TOP TEN

They are, in no particular order, consistently proving to be Elton John, Elvis, The Who, The Rolling Stones, Jimi Hendrix, The Beatles, Eric Clapton, Madonna, The Sex Pistols and Bob Dylan. I have dedicated two separate pieces later in this chapter to look more closely at Madonna and The Beatles.

Photographic document of The Rolling Stones by Gered Mankowitz,
signed by the photographer, £750

© Image Courtesy of Adrian Harrington Rare Books

Two rolls of promotional Sex Pistols Loo Paper sold in September 2003

at Sotheby's for £480 © Image Courtesy of Sotheby's

THE HEAVY HITTERS

The title king of the castle, for the moment at least, is jointly shared by Eric Clapton, Jimi Hendrix and Elvis Presley. In 1999, a world record was established for the sale of a guitar at auction. It was 'Brownie' – a 1956 Fender Stratocaster, and one of Eric Clapton's favourite guitars, used on the whole of the *Layla* album. It sold for £316,879.

However, in June 2004, 'Blackie', Clapton's other legendary guitar, a Stratocaster, went on sale at Christie's in New York. It shattered the existing world record by selling for a shade under $1 million!

Eric Clapton's 'Blackie' sold for $959,500

© Image Courtesy of Christie's Images Ltd. 2006

190

A few years ago, I was lucky enough to be able to take onto ITV1's *This Morning*, Jimi Hendrix's very own Flying V guitar called 'Flying Angel'.

This was used extensively in the studio and live at the Rainbow Bridge, Atlanta Pop, Isle of White and Paris Olympia concerts, among others. It was loaned to me by the Vault Museum at the Hard Rock Cafe in London. I managed to get presenters Phillip and Fern to play a 'guess the value' game. Phillip quite literally stumbled backwards when I revealed the insurance value, and he nearly knocked over John Lennon's *Hard Day's Night* premiere suit on a mannequin. The figure was £1 million!

Elvis may well be more collectable than even these guys. Ever since his death in 1977, the demand for his personal property has increased notably. His credit cards or even Graceland's CCTVs can now make thousands of pounds at auction.

One of Elvis's acoustic guitars was sold by Christie's in 1993 for a hip-shaking £99,000. In1999, a specific charity auction held in Las Vegas, now known as the 'Elvis Garage Sale', saw nearly 2,000 lots sell including a tiny guitar plectrum for $10,000, and his 1956 Lincoln car for $250,000!

Of course, there are literally millions of different items of memorabilia out there. One of the most dynamic developments has been the ability to trade on the Web. Here you can pick up all manner of pieces from belts and badges to records and posters. It has opened up rock and pop memorabilia collecting to a whole new generation. Prices for these sort of things, unless rare, tend to be most affordable.

Currently, the state of the market looks healthy in the popular merchandise and records field – spurned on by a combination of Internet auction sites trading globally and at the top end, as Christie's recently showed. If you are interested in getting it together and starting a collection, my best advice would be: to collect just one act otherwise you may well be overwhelmed; to pay a good auction house a visit and watch their next rock and pop sale – make a note of hammer prices in the catalogue so you know for the future and who knows, one day you might be standing there bidding on a Beatles guitar or a Busted drum set; and lastly, buy and collect what you like, and then you may well be surprised by their future values in years to come.

MADONNA

Long before Madge became a children's author, she burst onto the international collecting scene. Unlike so many other solo acts, Madonna has a timeless appeal and this has translated well into the secondary collecting market – it's not just fans who snap up items which relate to her and her music, it's also serious rock and pop memorabilia collectors worldwide. Madge is so collectable that there are guidebooks and web sites devoted exclusively to her merchandise – an honour usually reserved for bands that have long split up.

- At the top of any memorabilia tree are the sacred fruits – the original clothing, lyrics and instruments.
- I once took some of the great lady's clothing onto the *Channel Five News*. It was a stage outfit that a fan had found in a bin liner in the street after a gig. She phoned Madonna's management and they said she could keep it. It went under the hammer at Christie's for thousands!
- Other rarities to track down include her infamous *Sex* book. It is the unopened editions that now get collectors hot under the collar. It came in a silver foil pack and caused a thunderstorm at the time.
- The 12-inch picture disc version of her single 'Erotica', (which was suddenly withdrawn in Britain because of the naughty image), has also become a serious collectable and can swap hands for big money.

- Many promotional items produced for Madonna are of high quality and high desirability. Look for the particularly rare lava lamp and fibre lamp – both made for the *Ray of Light* album. These are inscribed and can make over £1,000 apiece.

- Top US jewellers Tiffany & Co. created engraved key fobs for the Drowned World Tour in 2001. Not surprisingly, these are Madonna must-haves.

THE BEATLES

It's nice to look at a group from the Rock and Roll past. At the very, very top of the collecting world, high above all others, stand the Fab Four. Clearly it is the global and timeless nature of the band and their wonderful music that makes them the subject of such adulation, but John's murder in 1980, the untimely death of George and even Paul's public divorce woes have, as collectors have come to expect, created even more interest in all things Fab.

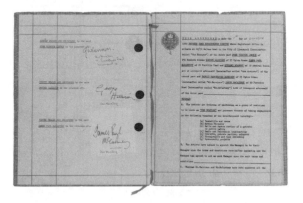

Rare signed copy of the revised management agreement between The Beatles and Brian Epstein. It sold for £122,850 in May 2005 at Christie's

© Image Courtesy of Christie's Images Ltd. 2006

The biggest interest usually comes from the States and Japan and it is fair to say, these serious fans have almost no limit to the amount they will spend to get hold of particularly special pieces for their, or their company's, collections.

I mentioned John's dinner suit from the premier of *A Hard Day's Night* on a 1960s special for *This Morning*. It had been lent to me via The Beatles Story Museum in Liverpool and was insured for around £55,000!

These Holy Grails belong in the exclusive territory of the international auction. In 1999 I recall the sale of the hand-written lyrics for the classic 'I am the Walrus' at Christie's. This single piece of paper with twenty lines of writing sold for an astonishing £78,500. John Lennon's Rolls Royce was sold by Sotheby's of New York in 1985 for £2.2 million. This of course was right at the dawn of the modern surge in interest in pop and rock memorabilia.

More recently, Christie's had their best-ever sale of pop memorabilia. Topping the bill was lot 128 – a signed copy of the revised management agreement between The Beatles and their manager Brian Epstein that was dated 1 October 1962, right at the dawn of their careers.

At the same sale, a custom-made Vox Kensington guitar sold for £117,250 with an estimate of £80,000–120,000. The guitar was used by John during the rehearsals for the 'Hello Goodbye' video filmed in London in November 1967 and was also used by George during rehearsals for 'I Am The Walrus' (for use in *The Magical Mystery Tour* film), filmed in Kent in September 1967.

Beatles on a Budget

You don't have to have a pay packet like a rock legend to afford some really Fab pieces of memorabilia.

- While recently recording an episode of *Everything Must Go!* in Nottingham, I watched a very fine poster with facsimile autographs, in good shape, and a lovely Irish Linen Beatles tea towel, unused and original 1960s, go under the hammer for £30 or so.
- If you can afford a grand or more, you still can find personal items: a library book signed out by Lennon from the Quarrybank School in 1954, complete with his class details, fetched £1,500 at Sotheby's a few years ago.
- These trays were from DJ Mike Reid's sale when I filmed *The Life Laundry* for BBC2. They are worth around £100–£150 as a group.

Beatles trays, £100–150

© Jamie Breese

Royal Doulton Beatles jugs

© Image Courtesy of Sotheby's

- The Beatles have been the subject of character or figural Jugs. In the early to mid-1980s, Royal Doulton made a lovely series. A set of four makes £400-600 right now.
- If you collect figurines/dolls then you are well catered for, too. Car Mascot Inc. created some of the best in 1964. Today, the 8-inch Bobbin' Head Beatles vary between £800 and £1,000 for mint and boxed sets. The larger versions are now considered even rarer.

A set of Beatles Bobbin' Head dolls sold in September 2003 for £960

© Image Courtesy of Sotheby's

Where to Find out More

- Christie's, South Kensington, 85 Old Brompton Road, London SW7 3LD. Tel: 020 7930 6074.
- Sotheby's, 34-35 New Bond Street, London W1A 2AA. Tel: 020 7293 5555.
- The Beatles Story is in the band's homeland, Albert Dock, Liverpool. Tel: 0151 709 1963.
- The Vault Museum at the Hard Rock Cafe in London. Tel: 020 7514 1704.

22

WHITEFRIARS GLASS

IN THE LAST ten years or so, there has been growing interest in the colourful world of studio glass. Names such as Vicke Lindstrand, and in particular, the creations of British factory Whitefriars, are all attracting attention.

The Studio Glass movement took off in Europe in the mid 1960s and had been developing in the USA since the 1950s. New technologies, the influences of everything from Pop Art to the atom, and the desire to get away from the austerity of wartime all went into the melting pot to create these distinctive wares.

The Scandinavians are usually the most well-known exponents of the craft, but Whitefriars is quickly catching up. This is good news as the firm is now defunct and there will be no more pieces made. Most

Meadow Green vase designed by Geoffrey Baxter with a Kingfisher vase, late 1960s

© Image Courtesy of Christie's Images Ltd. 2006

199

people who are familiar with the name will immediately think of the out-there work of 1960s designer and design director, Geoffrey Baxter. That is of course justified, but the company employed some of the finest glass designers of the age, including Barnaby Powell and William Wilson. The Powell furnaces had been going since the nineteenth century.

Today, there is clear evidence that the factory's output, at one point considered to be some of the very best in the world, is becoming a collectable to keep one's eye on. Prices on eBay have leveled out of late according to some experts. Certainly, a number of beady-eyed buyers have been making a mint.

HISTORY

Whitefriars started out in life in 1834 as James Powell & Sons. There had actually been glassmakers on their site since 1680. Powell wanted to establish a scheme to get his three sons up and going with a trade and despite having no real knowledge of glassmaking, they managed to gain a reputation as fine makers of stained glass comparatively quickly. This was helped by the big movement for new church construction in the Victorian age.

A big change came in the early 1860s after a series of fine pieces were made for the legendary William Morris building known as the Red House in Bexleyheath, Kent. The firm realised they could viably create tablewares for customers, albeit the wealthier members of society.

Large quantities of coloured glass were also produced for the needs of the Pre-Raphaelite painters, a highly influential movement of the era. This was taken further a decade later by scientist Harry James Powell, who spearheaded innovations in the development of glass and made sure the wares were appearing in as many of the new exhibitions as possible. Much of the firm's output ended up being of industrial and scientific use, such as thermometers.

The company rode the crest of the Art Nouveau era and later Art Deco movement, producing domestic pieces that reflected the exciting developments in fashion, architecture and design. There was also a move from central London to a new site near Harrow in 1923.

The Second World War and the demands of the war effort knocked the company back and it only really picked up again during the 1951 Festival of Britain. Whitefriars was able to capitalise on the event and build new business leads. All this was leading towards the 1960s and the radical new works overseen or directly created by Geoffrey Baxter.

The company as it was known closed down in October 1980. There were a whole host of reasons behind its sad demise: the stained glass department had closed in 1973, there were changes in the demand for industrial products and the general recession of the time made life difficult. The site of the factory in Harrow has been demolished, but the name lives on with the glassmaker Caithness who use the name for their paperweights.

A collection of late nineteenth- and early twentieth-century Whitefriars glass

© Image Courtesy of Sotheby's

HOW MUCH ARE THEY WORTH?

At the moment, the majority of the pieces from the 1960s are quite affordable.

- For example, a collector can pay between £30 and £50 and pick up a tidy Baxter piece such as the distinctive, textured 'Nailhead' vase (which stands 6¼in tall).
- A slightly bigger, more organic looking cased bowl from around 1965 commands anywhere from £60 to £160 from a good glassware dealer at present.
- If you are on a real budget, but want to secure a stylish piece now, then £20 to £40 will buy an attractive bud vase in blue or ruby.
- It is still quite possible to find good examples of Whitefriars glass at car-boot fairs. The season kicks off each year in April. Because many still see the collectable 1960s and 70s designs as either kitsch or zany, many car booters often overlook them.
- Best to do some research, perhaps buy a guide, so you know your patterns and shapes, and then get out there and start treasure hunting.

One thing I forgot to mention is that if you like distinctive, funky designs, then the Baxter-driven designs by Whitefriars look really great in the modern interiors of today's homes. In 2006, some experts reported that prices had dropped by up to a quarter using eBay prices paid as a guide.

GEOFFREY BAXTER

Baxter (1926–95) was Whitefriars' most famous and accomplished designer. He broke new ground with bold new innovations and helped the company recover from the austerity of post-war Britain and the changes made within the factory to accommodate the war effort.

He joined the factory in 1954, straight out of college. Baxter had studied at the prestigious Royal School of Art in London and was already showing promise. It is his work from the 1960s, most notably the very unusual Textured Range of wares, that are considered today must-haves by glass collectors. These were initially fashioned using all sorts of raw materials – from barbed wire to tree bark. The final pieces were produced in small quantities by moulding, so they are not one-offs, but there are enough of them around to make it possible to pick one up at auction for a reasonable amount.

If you are looking to make a mint, these could be worth stockpiling if you find them very cheaply. Remember, it is not a certainty, but is certainly one to watch.

Other works by Baxter, which are worth snapping up now if cheaply sourced, would include the unusually titled Drunken Bricklayer vases. These are tall pieces 13 inches high and come in several colours. These are currently increasing in value and most often command £1,000 or more in the best colours such as lilac.

THE BANJO VASE

- This vase, produced in 1967, is considered to be the finest design in the Textured Range.
- It is a large piece at around 13 inches in height and was initially available in three electric colours – the evocatively named willow, cinnamon and indigo. Slightly later, a few more colours appeared including kingfisher blue.
- Today, good, undamaged examples are sometimes being sold by top dealers for north of £1,000. A few years ago, you would have been lucky to get £100. It's an incredible surge in value and reflects the popularity and cult status of Baxter.

- If you can't afford this special piece, why not keep your eyes out for the Sunburst vase, also by Baxter. It's quite similar in appearance, around half the size but costs around £100.
- Again – a special tip off: these wares can still be found gracing the tables at car-boot fairs, charity shops and even hidden in job lots at your local auction rooms.

The Whitefriars Banjo vase

© Image Courtesy of Christie's Images Ltd. 2006

Where to Find out More

- There is a well-known book on the subject. Entitled *Whitefriars Glass: The Art of James Powell & Sons*, it is published by Richard Dennis Publications and is written by Lesley Jackson. It costs around £30.
- The Museum of London was given most of the records and archives before the quick demise of the company. They published a book on the subject.

23

CLARICE CLIFF

MANY ENTHUSIASTS AND design historians argue that Clarice Cliff was the leading light of the Art Deco era. The Deco style has never really been out of fashion since it burst onto the scene during the now legendary Exposition Internationale des Arts Décoratifs et Industriels Modernes which took place in Paris in 1925.

House and bridge teapot, £940

© Image Courtesy of Sotheby's

May Avenue charger, sold for £39,950

in 2003 at Christie's

© Image Courtesy of Christie's Images Ltd. 2006

THE ART DECO STYLE

Clarice was fortunate enough to attend the exhibition, and like all visitors witnessed a radical, fresh and modernist reaction to the far gentler, ornate, gothic-influenced Art Nouveau movement which had been dominant for the previous 30-odd years and had relied heavily on floral motifs and elegant images like butterflies and plant life.

Art Deco called less on nature and more on brightly coloured imagination and was heavily influenced by the exciting discoveries in the world of Egyptology, abstract art – most notably Picasso and the Cubists – as well as the music of the era, jazz.

Though the excitement had started to wane by the late 1930s, Deco's influence continues to this day and goes through revival after revival. The term Art Deco was coined as late as the mid-sixties and today, Clarice Cliff, the so-called Sunshine Girl, has become synonymous with that most exciting period.

HISTORY

Many of you will know her story – Clarice Cliff is today celebrated as a powerful female in what was still a totally male dominated industry. Women were the paintresses, not the managers, art directors or factory bosses. Through sheer hard work, Cliff lifted herself above her relatively poor circumstances in Stoke-on-Trent to get work at the nearby Wilkinson pottery in 1916.

It was during these early years that young Clarice caught the attention of the Wilkinson owners. In a legendary lucky break, she was given her very own studio in the newly acquired Newport Pottery. The aptly named, revolutionary range, which was to put Clarice's name on the international map from 1927 onwards, was simply called Bizarre. Amazingly, this was actually the result of an experiment – the factory had given her several hundred blank, old pieces and left her to it!

As her 'golden era' of design was ending in the early forties, she married her then boss Colley Shorter and they moved to the splendid Chetwynd House to the west of Stoke, famous for its gardens – a source of inspiration for Clarice.

Clarice was also a prolific designer. During her reign she managed to create over 2,000 different patterns, many of which were bold for their time, and over 500 different shapes.

A Clarice Cliff castellated circle

Isis jug £2,520

© Image Courtesy of Sotheby's

For me, when I think of her work, I remember the solid triangular handles that appear on many of the classic cups. This is the epitome of Art Deco, and despite having questionable functionality they must have been the talk of any tea party in their day.

Some of her most sought-after pieces include the fabulous May Avenue charger that sold at Christie's in London a few years ago. This particular pattern was produced very briefly in 1932 and 1933 and depicts a black-stemmed tree with green café-au-lait foliage alongside a rising avenue of red-roofed houses and spade-shaped trees. The chargers themselves are extremely rare but this was the largest charger size at a whooping 18 inches in diameter. The estimate was set at between £10,000 and £15,000 but on the day it went under the hammer for a world-record price at auction for any of her pieces – £39,950. This figure was double the previous record for any item by Cliff and made the headlines around the world.

OTHER CLARICE GEMS

- The Summerhouse pattern sugar sifter is another Clarice rarity. An identical sifter in, say, the Crocus pattern usually commands around £100. A Summerhouse version sold recently for a record £5,200 at Lyon & Turnbull auctioneers in Edinburgh.
- Clarice branched out in 1933 into more unfamiliar territory with a whole number of delicate wall masks and medallions – some of these were produced in very small numbers and often appear at the best sales with high estimates.
- Coffee services in ultra rare patterns such as Palermo are now desperately sought-after by Clarice Cliff fans.

CLARICE TODAY

The Clarice Cliff magic touch continued until around 1964 when her name stopped appearing on the factory wares. Her husband's death saw Clarice sell up the two firms to Midwinter's pottery and she went into retirement to be among the flowers which had so inspired her greatest designs.

In 1972, following the first-ever exhibition of her work in Brighton, Clarice passed away. At the same time, there was a groundswell of international interest developing in the collecting and antique world, and the rest is history.

Today, Cliff has a celebrated following with whole auctions dedicated to her wares. There are many reasons for her unique success: she was brighter and perhaps bolder than her female contemporaries Shelly and

Cooper; her ceramics were always offbeat; every piece is an almost unique object with the various items looking particularly great in groups.

Clarice's life was full of zest and she used her phenomenal skills, including marketing, to become a true pioneer of the potteries and went on to sell her iconic wares all over the world.

THE AGE OF JAZZ FIGURINES

Right at the top of most Clarice Cliff collectors' wish lists are these ultra-rare figurines. Designed in 1930 as table centrepieces or for placing on the wireless, the collection comprised five different figures, including a dancing couple, a banjo player and pianist.

Visually, they are perhaps less striking than a large plate or mask – they

Wedgwood Age of Jazz reproduction with another figurine, £329

© Image Courtesy of Christie's Images Ltd. 2006

are only a few inches high and flat sided – but they are certainly bright and colourful. They were introduced to the market right in the middle of the Great Depression and simply failed to sell that well, a factor that of course means there are far fewer around today to collect. Being so delicate, many surviving pieces are damaged and this has helped to push up the prices for mint examples.

Values obviously vary according to the condition and the actual shape. Most important Clarice sales will feature at least one. Christie's have seen their share: for example, an oboe and drummer version made just under £14,000 in 1997 while another sold for £15,525 in February 2000. This is not bad money for an almost experimental series, many of which ended up being disposed of due to poor sales.

If you'd rather not part with these amounts, you can keep your eyes peeled for the Wedgwood reproduction figurines. In 1996, the firm made just 150 limited editions of these fabulous figures. These were hand-painted like the originals. If you find a boxed example today, expect to pay £300–500. There have been more limited editions made recently and you can find these online for under £100 in many cases.

Where to Find out More

- Christie's and Sotheby's along with many other auction houses have had some superb sales of Clarice Cliff items in the past.
- Christie's, South Kensington 85 Old Brompton Road, London SW7 3LD. Tel: 020 7930 6074, www.christies.com.
- Sotheby's, 34-35 New Bond Street, London W1A 2AA. Tel: 020 7293 5000, www.sothebys.com.

24

BAKELITE RADIOS

IN THE LAST few years, you can't help but notice the appearance of what appear to be vintage radios for sale up and down the high street. Closer inspection reveals that these are in fact modern reproductions of some of the most fondly remembered sets from the 1950s and early 60s: the Roberts and Bush models are particularly striking.

It's nice to see a nod to the past, especially as many of these now work with FM and often digital, but I wonder if anybody in these companies has had the foresight to look back in time, just a little further, to the 1930s and 40s: to the golden era of radio and in particular, radio design.

I have a particular connection with these communication icons: in December 1998, I auditioned

Ecko AC74, 1933, £250–350

© Image Courtesy of On The Air Ltd.

for a presenting role on BBC2's flagship series, *The Antiques Show*. I had to stand in an antiques arcade in Bristol, and talk about one item in front of a camera. I borrowed my father's Philco Radio and because I was passionate, I think that swung the job for me. There began my TV and writing career: so I bought my own set last year to remind me!

HISTORY

The first broadcasts were made by the BBC in the early 1920s and owning a wireless set soon became the norm. It became crucial during the war years.

There are so many types of radio that I have chosen to focus on one variety – those made from Bakelite. Phenol formaldehyde is the technical term for most Bakelite. It was first patented in 1907. It's a plastic that requires great heat and pressure to form and once formed, it's set for life. Great for radios.

From the 1920s onwards, mass manufacture and modernity ushered-in a brave new world, and Bakelite, effectively the original plastic, was at the forefront of this race to design democracy. For the first time, everyone could have their own, stylish, camera, radio or even a toaster. It was rightly called 'the material of a thousand uses' and what's more, it was cheap!

The Depression in the US and Britain forced designers to come up with simple and economical shapes. This, together with the restrictions

GEC BC4941, 1948, £100–150

© Image Courtesy of On The Air Ltd.

of the actual moulding process, contributed to the streamlined, Art Deco look of that era.

As a result of the early 1990s surge of interest in all things Bakelite, many radios (British and US) made before 1955 have become sought-after and some examples are particularly desirable. The values to be honest do vary considerably according to condition and demand – and demand did peak a few years back.

Bush DAC90, 1946, £50–80

© Image Courtesy of On The Air Ltd.

You don't have to spend a lot of money to acquire a good vintage radio. The popular DAC 90, made by Bush, is a familiar sight at many car-boot fairs and you may get lucky and find one for a few pounds. A nice clean brown or black example could command £70 from a dealer and the cream alternative is slightly harder to come by.

At the top end of the market lies a mixture of British and US design. The American Air King radios, which are not dissimilar to the 1930s skyscrapers, came in a variety of great colours. For many collectors this is the greatest small radio design of all time. Prices today fluctuate according to the motif above the dial e.g. Egyptian or Clock. In the past, some models have made over £2,500.

ECKO RADIOS

The famous round radios from the British firm EK Cole are also desirable. All Ekco radios are sought-after by collectors, but the Art Deco-inspired round models have proved the most enduring.

They all have rather dull model numbers such as AD65 and so forth, but the actual appearance of the cabinets is truly remarkable. There were also a few special-edition coloured examples manufactured for trade fairs or made specially to order. When these have come up for sale they have made several thousand pounds.

Perhaps best of all is the grand looking Ekco All Electric Consolette Model RS3 designed by J White. Built and manufactured in 1931, this radio was ground-breaking in that it was the very first English radio cabinet to have been made entirely from Bakelite. This truly would have been the pride and joy of any family at the time. Today, prices vary, but a good set can cost hundreds from a specialist dealer.

By the mid 1950s, newer, brighter materials like Styrene and Formica came to prominence. Bakelite was used less, while the sets of the golden days reminded people of the hardships of the war years. Sony released the small transistor radio and the rest is history. It did appear that the best designs were saved for Bakelite.

Ecko A22, 1946, £600–800

© Image Courtesy of On The Air Ltd.

THE PHILCO PEOPLE'S SET

This is a Philco radio set. It is one of my favourite collectables of all time and rightly has pride of place in my lounge. It is known as The People's Set and was designed with the intention of producing a set cheap enough for the general public to afford. Made from Bakelite, it is a solid, well-designed and still very useable antique.

The People's Set first arrived in 1936. The initial cost was around 6 guineas (£6 6s) which really wasn't an arm and a leg in those days. Several different versions were made available – a black or a dark brown cabinet and either mains or battery operated. There was also a radiogram model (hard to find today) which was wooden and featured a gramophone as well as a receiver. Lastly, at the time, a customer could order a Deluxe model that sported a wooden cabinet and was far more expensive.

Even though this radio was mass-produced, there are comparatively few in truly mint condition. One thing that helps large radios like this is that they tended to be kept in one place only and not moved about. Try and avoid a damaged model if you have the opportunity to buy one. What really makes this set desirable is the fact that is a design masterpiece: it's a great example of the streamlined, cleanlined Art Deco look that was all the rage in the 1920s and 30s. The Art Deco movement borrowed from a whole number of different styles including

Philco People's Set, 1930s, £350–450

© Jamie Breese

Egyptian and Cubist art and is evident, here, in this icon of consumer goods. You can read a little bit more about this look in the chapter about Clarice Cliff.

In terms of price, wooden radios seem to be less desirable in general and today a Deluxe model can cost as little as £60. However, a good Bakelite example in original condition will cost around £350–450. A specialist can often supply a less complete model for £300–350.

Ecko SH25, 1932, £350–500

© Image Courtesy of On The Air Ltd.

Ecko AC97, 1936, £350–450

© Image Courtesy of On The Air Ltd.

Where to Find out More

- Readers can contact On The Air. They are specialist dealers with whom I've dealt with before and they are friendly and reliable. Tel: 01244 530 300, www.vintageradio.co.uk.
- The Bakelite Museum in Williton, West Somerset have a selection of 400 Bakelite radios including many of those mentioned here. www.bakelitemuseum.co.uk. Tel: 01984 632 133. (Open Easter – September. No valuation requests please!)

25

ROYAL DOULTON FIGURINES

THEY ARE COLOURFUL, lively, fairly sturdy and utterly collectable. Of course, for some, these will appear slightly twee and are perhaps for a certain customer only. But Royal Doulton products command a huge international fan base, particularly the United States where many things which are considered classically British sell rather well. Many designs are produced in fairly small runs, which bolsters the value down the line on many pieces. If you know where to look, these classic figurines are a consideration if you have the time to make a mint.

HN2826, Leda and the Swan. Part of a series of four and valued at around £8,000

© Image Courtesy of Royal Doulton

HISTORY

Royal Doulton is one of the most recognisable brand names in the world. The firm was founded by John Doulton in 1815 when he first set up shop in Lambeth. It became 'Royal' at the beginning of the twentieth century when King Edward granted the company permission to use the coveted title in recognition of the quality of its work.

HN1221, Lady Jester, £2,820

© Image Courtesy of Sotheby's

The company's fortunes have changed over the years – they used to employ thousands of some of the most skilled craftsmen in Europe, but the simple, sad fact remains that today, the majority of people do not take tea or eat at the table like they used to. This has had an affect on all the potteries of course. The company remains, however, a world leader and is a name that truly helps to put the Great into Great Britain.

One of the most timeless and successful ranges that any pottery has pulled off are the Doulton figurines.

CLASSIC COLLECTABLES

They remain classic examples of twentieth-century collectables, which are now beginning to be classed as antiques. The good news is that figurines are still being made, are still affordable and many represent sound investments. There are characters for every taste and pocket on the collectables market, most falling into the £100–350 bracket from a dealer, and today, over 4,000 different studies have been created.

The figurines first appeared on St George's day 1913 following a visit to the Doulton factory by King George V and Queen Mary (who was a regular visitor, no doubt because she was always provided with vast dinner services and the like!). The queen was supposedly visiting the factory and remarked on what a 'Darling' the first figure produced was, (pictured here). It was originally entitled 'Bedtime', but this was quickly changed to commemorate HRH's comment.

DATING AND IDENTIFICATION

Dating and identification of each piece is fortunately quite easy with the clear HN registration number on the base of most figurines.

This was a device employed by the senior painter, Harry Nixon, who realised that this new range would need to be carefully catalogued.

The HN number was the honour bestowed upon him and remains in use to this day. The first figure, Darling, therefore, bears the registration number HN 1.

Darling, the first HN figurine

© Image Courtesy of Royal Doulton

CONTEMPORARY PIECES

Of course, Doulton figurines are still in production and new ranges are constantly appearing each year. One of the most ambitious figurines ever made by the company was St George (HN 4371). This was one of the most complex pieces the studio had ever created and the head modeller, Alan Maslankowski, spent over three months getting it right. It came out in 2004 in an extremely limited edition of just 50, standing over 17in tall and costing an awesome £10,000. Doulton told me that they have all sold which tells us a lot about their collectablity.

A more affordable piece would be the HM Queen Elizabeth II Coronation (HN 4476) that was produced by Pauline Parsons to commemorate the 50th anniversary of Her Majesty's Coronation. Still limited to the more familiar 2,000 pieces, it cost around £275 new. In 1973 Royal Doulton produced a limited edition Coronation Figurine to celebrate 20 years of Her Majesty's reign: now it can make up to £1,500!

PIECES FROM THE PAST

HN 2827, Juno and the Peacock

© Image Courtesy of Royal Doulton

HN 2828, Europa and the Bull

© Image Courtesy of Royal Doulton

Sunshine Girl sold in June 2005 at

Sotheby's for £2,400

© Image Courtesy of Sotheby's

This Royal Doulton piece sold at

Sotheby's for £3,525 in May 2002

© Image Courtesy of Sotheby's

The most excitement comes with the figurines from the past. Prices do tend to vary enormously according to the character, the amount produced and other factors such as quality of the paintwork. The famous Old Balloon Seller (HN 1315) from 1929 makes between £125–185 while the Myths and Maidens Set (pieces HN 2825–9) from 1982–6 has been valued at over £8,000.

One of the rarest of all the Doulton figurines is also holding balloons; she is called 'Folly' and has an Art Deco look and a conical hat. In the past she has made over £2,300. Even better, the Sunshine Girl, from 1929 (pictured) can make thousands. Very few figurines can be found for under £100 and they have covered every conceivable subject from history to sport; from personalities to folkloric characters.

It is worth bearing in mind the other ranges of collectable figures that Royal Doulton has produced in case you come across any on your travels.

- The famous Bunnykins figures, which first appeared in 1939 and were inspired by the drawings of the daughter of the managing director of Royal Doulton.
- Up until recently, Snowman figures were very hot. Twenty-three different figures were made between 1985 and 1994 and they cost around £12 each. In recent years these have been snowballing – the skiing figure commands £400, but a few years ago he was twice as dear!
- For most collectors (and me!) the real appreciation comes with admiring the piece itself. Each one is a work of care, attention and detail and it wouldn't surprise me if Doulton make it to £10,000! so much more than an investment opportunity.

Lady and the Unicorn

© Image Courtesy of Royal Doulton

THE OLD BALLOON SELLER

This charming, colourful piece is quite possibly one of the most recognisable collectables ever produced. Called simply The Old Balloon Seller, she has been a centrepiece in many homes around the world for over 75 years. She bears the all-important HN number 1315 and was one of a series of streetseller figurines that Royal Doulton produced.

The Old Balloon Seller was created by Doulton legend Leslie Harradine and was first released back in 1929. The earlier pieces were earthenware, but in the mid 1960s, they were made with English translucent china – or porcelain. In 1998, this piece was sadly discontinued but her uniqueness has meant she has the accolade of being one of the longest-running figurines that the firm has ever produced.

The seller is one of several to look out for, so she appeals to the collector: Balloon Man was also designed by Harradine and is worth between £140–70. The Old Balloon Seller is seen as a must-have, which completes any collection, though she is not too hard to find today in good condition. You might pay anywhere between £125–85 for a nice, clean example from an antique dealer today. There is also a special version produced in a different colour for a series of events in 1999 and it commands around £150–200 at present.

If you are beady-eyed, she and others like her can still be found in charity shops and other cheaper places!

HN 1315, The Old Balloon Seller

© Image Courtesy of Royal Doulton

Where to Find out More

- The Royal Doulton International Collectors' Club (membership info 01782 404046). There are factory tours available at Barlaston, where you can see the visit the studios and factory shop:
- The Wedgwood Visitor Centre, Barlaston, Stoke-on-Trent, Staffordshire ST12 9ES. Bookings and Information: Mon – Fri: 01782 282 986 Sat & Sun: 01782 282452, www.royaldoulton.com, email: bookings@wedgwood.com,
- Sotheby's, 34-35 New Bond Street, London W1A 2AA. Tel: 020 7293 5555

26

BARBIE AND ACTION
MAN... AND SINDY

It is one of the strange quirks of the collectables market that something such as a plastic doll barely 50 years old can, in some cases, be perceived as more valuable than some of the finest nineteenth-century pieces we have looked at.

Dolls are of course one of the most fondly cherished antiques and they date back several thousand years to the ancient Greeks. All sorts of materials have been used from wax and papier-mâché to contemporary plastics. What changed the market forever was the appearance of a certain teenage doll at a toy fair in New York in 1959.

Barbie number 1

© Image Courtesy of PA Photos

227

Barbie was forever ingrained in world culture from that moment and she has now sold over one billion clones of herself and been reincarnated more times than The Doctor. But the toy market is fiercely competitive and it was only a short while before a male doll was born. Action Man wasn't the first, but he is the most enduring – the question is, who, in today's collecting market, is best?

BARBIE

Barbie was the brainchild of Ruth and Elliot Handler who founded toy giant Mattel. In the late 1950s they made the first doll for their daughter, Barbara. This first ever model would have set a parent back around $3.

How do you spot a number 1 today?
- She was sporting a black-and-white striped swimsuit.
- She had her hair in a blonde ponytail.
- Her irises were white.
- She had pointy eyebrows and holes in her feet!

There were four other editions of this first model, each one changed very slightly. Boxed and mint examples today are exceptionally hard to locate. Several thousand pounds is required to add an unboxed number 1 to your collection. After proving an instant hit in 1959, she reappeared in Gay Parisienne and *Roman Holiday* glad rags. There was a whole number of snazzy outfits available in the first year alone. Not surprisingly, it is mainly adults who can afford these early treasures.

There are of course plenty of dolls to seek out for collectors on a limited budget and the Web is a good trading post. No collection would be complete without Ken, Barbie's steadfast and utterly loyal boyfriend. They both have defied the ageing process and still find time to do all those outdoor pursuits. Ken first came on the scene in 1960 and was named after Ruth and Elliot's son.

Many collectors suggest that the key collecting development came in 1980 with the first Barbie National Convention. Many of the earliest owners had now grown up and Barbie, of course, symbolised their lost innocence and nostalgia for youth. Since then, there have been a number of limited edition or collector ranges such as Blue Rhapsody Barbie, porcelain versions and depictions of her as characters from TV series.

There have been several notable auctions where her wares have been touted for sale – and some have been very exclusive indeed. In fact, a famous auction house once offered a spectacular one-off model created specifically for Barbie's 40th anniversary. This featured real diamonds and the estimate featured many zeros!

ACTION MAN

So what about the guys then? The key influence in the creation and marketing of the first Action Man was the US-produced GI Joe doll, launched in 1964. Our chap was a homegrown 12-inch hero made by Leicester-based Palitoy. He first stormed the toyshops of Britain in January 1966. He initially had a rival in Tommy Gunn made by rival Pedigree, but Action Man won the first and decisive battle and Tommy quickly bit the dust.

Talking Commander, second issue. Sold in June 2005 for £120

© Image Courtesy of Vectis Auctions Ltd.

Unsurprisingly, the first dolls are more valuable, with the vintage era considered to run from 1966–84. You should always look for boxed and preferably mint examples with the flesh-coloured groin area – the later issues sported blue pants. The basic early toy was articulated with 21 joints. Also, the earlier models (until 1972) had solid plastic ungripping hands, (rather than the later flexible rubber fingers), and painted-on hair as opposed to felt.

The Talking Commander doll from 1968 now commands around the £300 – 400 mark. Even later dolls such as the Helicopter Pilot model from 1973 will currently set you back around £250.

In general, the vintage Action Man has a military bearing. There are exceptions, though. There were a number of sportsmen including footballers. Also look out for Indian Brave, Captain Zargon (an alien) and the hard to find Action Girl!

Action Man was well catered for on the accessory front and some complete, rare sets (usually card mounted) are worth more than the dolls today.

As a kid, I remember the action vehicles being expensive at the time. I had a handful of lucky friends whose parents could afford the tanks, boats and helicopters. Nowadays, you often see the tanks at car boots, but they are usually battered and only worth picking up in case they have rare bits and pieces swilling around inside.

In 1984, following many missions and overwhelmed by enemy *Star Wars* toys, Action Man had to go AWOL. In the 1990s he reemerged and underwent a huge rebranding exercise – a gamble that seems to have paid off for new owners Hasbro. The military theme was downplayed and extreme activities and modern fashions were taken into account, so he was sold with kit like mountain bikes and F1 cars. Some vintage collectors see this as selling out and an unnecessary softening of his image!

Like Barbie, there are some very rare models that collectors covet. These are just not in the same price category as her early or rare editions, however. For example, the sentry box guards such as The Royal Guard (wearing a blue and white outfit) can make £1,500–1,800 if boxed and mint. Prices tend to fluctuate and it's worth researching the market thoroughly before making any big outlays.

Condition really is everything with Action Man. Books exist to help the novice through this minefield. Plenty of items sell on the web and there are many dedicated collectors' fairs in this country. When push comes to shove, in terms of sheer, outright collectability and value, the glamour and creature comforts of Barbie's World win hands down.

THE RIVAL: SINDY

The fashion doll market isn't too crowded, but there is only one serious rival to the throne that Barbie has sat atop so comfortably for the last five decades in terms of the collectables market. Our Brit kid Sindy has been in the shadows for some time, but she is starting to be taken seriously as collectable in her own right.

It was the British toy firm, Pedigree who brought Sindy to life in 1963. In the mid–1980s, toy giant Hasbro took over. By that time, there had been a wealth of

Pedigree Sindy doll, 1963. This was sold at Vectis Auctions in July 2005 for £260

© Image Courtesy of Vectis Auctions Ltd

outfits, accessories and play-sets produced and collectors today look for boxed items in the very best condition.

No teenage fashion doll would be complete without an optional fella – in this case her boyfriend, the puzzlingly, conventionally named Paul. You'd imagine something like Kurt or Brad!

Sindy also had a sister but in this case she bore the cross of the name Patch. All these extra characters add to collectability, of course, and traditionally these less-important extras sold less well, so are harder to acquire in A1 condition today. Sindy even had her very own TV studio action set!

What's Hot?

- Most collectors will look to acquire a Number One issue Sindy. You'll need to research this before taking the plunge – sites such as eBay.co.uk are good to look at to get a handle on current values – there are different hair colours on this rare doll.
- Toy auctioneers Vectis made a big noise in July 2006 when a Pedigree Walking Sindy (pictured overleaf) from 1970, made £820 against an estimate of £40–60!
- Look too for Sindy's other friends: Gayle makes up to a few hundred in mint condition; her French buddy Mitzi (pictured) with blonde locks is possibly the most valuable character.
- Even the distinctly un-British McDonalds Sindy doll from the 1980s is now collectable!

Pedigree Walking Sindy doll from 1970, sold at Vectis Auctions in July 2004 for £820

© Image courtesy of Vectis Auctions Ltd.

Pedigree Mitzi doll, £150

© Image courtesy of Vectis Auctions Ltd.

Where to Find out More

- If you are just starting out in collecting or interested in seeing the array of different models on a year-by-year timeline, then take a look online at www.barbiecollectibles.com.
- www.barbie.com is the official site which is aimed mainly at young people and there's less to glean about her collectable status.

27

SINCLAIR COLLECTABLES

IF YOU ARE interested in collecting, then you won't have missed the appearance of a few colourful retro electronics books on the shelves of your favourite bookshop. Retro is so new-fangled and fresh that the market and the guidebooks can hardly keep up with the new developments.

Did you know that recent technology could be a really great area to make a mint? If you didn't know this then neither will the car-boot stallholders or many of those using online auction sites!

I am going to let you in on another little secret: one which should enable you to go out, right now, and make profits on anything you find cheaply. In this chapter, we turn back the hands of time just a little to find ourselves in the late 1970s and early 80s. A world full of digital promise and ripe with the possibilities afforded by the microchip. Leading the way in western Europe was a great man with a great mind – a true individual whose prolific work has left us today with a legacy of suddenly quite collectable icons.

SIR CLIVE SINCLAIR

Sir Clive Sinclair was born in 1940. He is still working on projects to this day through his company Sinclair Research. Not content with being a unique voice in technology, he went on to become a chairman of British Mensa in 1980 (he has an IQ of 159, incidentally). What made him so special is his focus on miniaturisation. Sir Clive was behind many electronic world firsts too: the hard-to-find executive calculator from 1972 and the first LED digital watch in 1975, called the Sinclair Black Watch.

In more recent years, despite not having his name on so many ground-breaking artefacts, his interest in mobility and miniaturisation continues with his Z1 radio, promoted as the world's smallest radio – costing a tiny £9.95 – and the lightest personal sea propeller in the world in the form of the SEA-DOO seascooter (this costs from £350). Whether these become collectables of the future is crystal ball gazing but radios have a good track record to date.

It's true that many of the current retro/Sinclair treasure hunters in the know are males in the their thirties, seeking to recapture their youth, but Sir Clive's treasures should also appeal to those who have an interest in collectables in general as this is actually one of the cutting edges of the used goods market. It gives an indication of how something becomes iconic and how quickly objects perceived to have little value can so suddenly be traded on the Internet for many hundreds of pounds.

THE C5 ELECTRIC TRIKE

An iconic oddity of the 1980s is this ground-breaking three wheeler – the Sinclair C5. It was revealed to an unsuspecting world in 1985 and remained in production for just one and half years. Yet Sinclair still managed to sell many thousands around the world. Today, C5s in fine condition are worth surprisingly large sums of money.

Despite the rumours and bad press, there was no record of anyone having had a serious accident; they were sold originally for as little as

Sir Clive demonstrating the C5 Electric Trike

© Image Courtesy of PA Photos

£200; you didn't need a driving licence to drive one and, indeed, some have argued that it was not only a real attempt at electric power but also ahead of its time in terms of thinking about the environment.

The C5 had a top speed of 15 mph with a claimed range of about 20 miles on one charge. This turned out to be more like 10 miles. The vehicle also had a supplementary pedal drive for extra power to get up steep hills. They can be specially modified from a 12volt to a 24volt system, thereby doubling the speed for off-road use.

Adam Harper is the official supplier of parts. He was also a judge on the BBC's *Robot Wars* for several seasons, and has always been a C5 restorer and parts dealer. Once he modified a C5 to achieve a speed of and 150 mph and broke the world electric vehicle land speed record!

Many C5s sold abroad, in particular Italy where scooter culture is far more dominant. As a result, despite the thousands made, they are reasonably scarce in the UK. Many models have fallen into a state of disrepair or been destroyed. Their value at the time was probably undermined by a bout of unfavourable publicity. People treat objects with less care when something is perceived to be relatively worthless.

Today, it is interesting to see the release of machines such as the Segway taking off. This two-wheeled electric 'scooter' is even selling to Police Departments in the US with a price tag of just under £5,000. The C5 cost £399 at most.

- A standard C5, in okay condition and missing its box, might sell for £500–800.
- If boxed, in fine condition and with the optional accessories (such as wing mirrors, safety flag and raincover), specialist auctions sell them for around £600–1,500.

SINCLAIR TV

Sir Clive made a substantial contribution to the world of television, too. He released the world's first multi-standard 'pocket' TV in 1977. This was called the Microvision MTV 1. A few years later came a reduced price version which sold for £99.95. You can find out more in the chapter dedicated to collectable TV.

The mini TV that more people will be familiar with is the multi-standard flat-screen FTV 1. More like a TV Walkman, it was released in September 1983 and cost £79.95. I love the classic red and black 1980s looks. Today, the Microvision MTV 1 in mint condition can now command between £400 and £600. The FTV 1 sold more units so is currently cheaper to pick up – around £100 from web auctions is about right.

HOME COMPUTERS

In the early 1980s, Sinclair Research took the lead in the personal computer market. Sir Clive always had serious intentions for his small wonderboxes: to encourage the man in the street to have a crack at programming. Without a doubt, the majority of his computers ended up as games consoles.

Sinclair ZX80 computer, £500–1,000

© Jamie Breese

Most collectable right now is the ultra-rare ZX80. This tiny white box went on sale in February 1980 in kit (for you to make yourself at home) and ready-made form. Both machines retailed for under £100: astonishingly cheap compared to the competition. The ZX80 had a miniscule one kilobyte of RAM. Before production ended in August 1981, 100,000 units had been sold.

Interestingly, there were some ZX80 clones made. These show a white text on a black background on their displays and are worth less. Currently, the best figure I've seen paid for a boxed, original ZX80 with the manual has been £900. Online they sell for £250–500 mint and boxed on average. I paid two quid for one at a car boot in East London in the early 90s! If you want to see a ZX80, one is currently on display at London's Science Museum.

The immediate successor was the black boxed ZX81 in March 1981 – seen as an advance by being cheaper at £69.95. With a clock speed of just 3.5 MHz (today's PCs are more like 3.5 GHz!), this sold an amazing one million units in its first two years. Then in 1982 came the revolutionary, squelchy-keyed, colour Spectrum. A mint, boxed ZX81 might fetch £70-100 currently, whilst a Spectrum could probably pull in around £100.

CALCULATORS

Another collectable Sinclair to keep your eyes peeled for is The Executive. This was first introduced in 1972 and was the world's first truly pocket-sized calculator. It sold originally for £79 and earned over £2.5 million in export revenue. Now, it can be found on display at the Museum of Modern Art in New York and can easily fetch a hundred on the Web.

Where to Find out More

- You can find out more about Sir Clive and his products by visiting www.sinclair-research.co.uk.
- One of the leading authorities on Sinclair collectables, Enrico Tedeschi, has written a book. *Sinclair Archaeology* is a complete photo guide to the Sinclair world and costs around £14. (Published by Hove Books, ISBN: 0 9527883 0 6.)
- For authorised Sinclair C5 spares, repair, upgrades and restoration, contact Adam Harper. Tel: 07889 646 009 or visit: www.sinclair-research.co.uk/c5.php

28

JAMES BOND
COLLECTABLES

Aston Martin Vanquish © Image Courtesy of L Tilley/Corgi Classics Ltd.

2006 was of added excitement for cinemagoers as Bond came back…and with a new face. Many have argued that the super-cool Pierce Brosnan was the best since Connery and some have declared he would be a hard act to follow. *Casino Royale* was the first outing for Daniel Craig… and he was a huge hit as Bond.

All the speculation only served to renew interest in what most would argue is the most popular movie franchise of all time. As a result, the 007 series has also proven to have the most enduring appeal for collectors. Recent success, fuelled by previous international 007 auction sales, trading on the web, affordability for the beginner and a steady increase in value from the smallest toy to the most fabulous movie prop, makes 007 collecting so much fun.

Sorry to dash your hopes from the outset, but if you dream of making a mint from a real movie-used prop, costume or vehicle, then in all likelihood you'll most likely be needing a pay packet like a Hollywood star in order to buy into this upper storey of the memorabilia market. For example, my favourite auction item came up for sale in 1998. It was the actual steel-rimmed hat that Goldfinger's footsoldier Oddjob threw as a weapon. It was a real highlight piece at the sale with a whole page of pictures and description in the catalogue. An iconic prop from the most iconic Bond movie, it sold for £62,000. The equally iconic beachwear of a certain Pussy Galore in the very first Bond, *Dr No*, also made similar headlines when it was sold for £35,000.

It's not just the pieces from the early Connery era that capture the headlines when they appear for sale at auction. A stunt gun from the Brosnan movie *Tomorrow Never Dies* sold for twice its estimate of £4,250 and his screen-worn wristwatch in *GoldenEye*, went for around £6,000.

A few years ago, a huge number of lots were sold in London at Fleetwood Owen auctions. There was a cracking variety of gems to bid for which suited every pocket, including the modestly priced radioactive barrel prop, at £100.

One of the surprises of 2004 was the hammer price on a single model boat used in the classic *The Spy Who Loved Me*. The auctioneers had set an estimate of £1,200–1,500 but it eventually sold for several times that at an amazing £7,170 – a good example of what happens if fans just have to have it. This is also a good example of when trying to make a mint from a specialist auction can be most tricky. For more on bidding and other auction aspects, take a look in the relevant chapter in the previous section.

If you are happy to collect much smaller props, which are still screen used, then you could go for one of the casino chips used in the 1989 movie *License To Kill*. It is sold together with a copy of a scene still from the film showing Timothy Dalton as Bond at the casino, and Fraser's Autographs were recently asking for around £160.

No write up about Bond memorabilia would be complete without a peek at the legendary vehicles. The ultimate car has to be the silver DB5 Aston Martin. A few years ago, a British businessman paid £157,750 for a 1965 DB5 that was driven by Pierce Brosnan in *GoldenEye*. This was a Valentine's Day gift for his wife! I used to have this habit of buying my mum CDs at Christmas which I actually wanted to listen to myself… I wonder?

Aston Martin DB5 © Image Courtesy of L Tilley/Corgi Classics Ltd.

CORGI ASTON MARTIN DB5

Top dog in most collectors' minds must be the suave superhero's very own spy car. The silver or gold Aston Martin DB5 is one of the most recognisable movie vehicles around and has stood the test of time in the public and the collectors' imaginations.

- Voted 'Toy of the Year' by the Toy Retailers Association in 1965, the company went on to sell over 3 million of them. 1965 was a great year for Corgi.

- The definitive find would be a mint and boxed silver car (it was also sold in gold), clean and complete with the special 'Secret Instructions' booklet.

- Another must-have that builds up the toy's value is the concertina-like 'Model car makers to James Bond' pamphlet and the presence of the Korean agent in the lethal passenger seat.

Aston Martin DB5, £350–500 © Image Courtesy of Corgi Classics Ltd.

- You would need to be on the salary of a movie star to buy a top nick DB5: currently they sell for anywhere from £350 up to £500 on a good day.
- Never one to miss a trick, Corgi have recently produced an accurate copy of their original 1965 car, available for about £7.50.

OTHER BOND GOODIES

When it comes to mega bucks, the £271,000 that was paid in 2000 for the *Goldfinger* 1937 Phantom III Rolls-Royce, seems to win the day.

More recently, Christie's sold the giant Moon Buggy from the film *Diamonds Are Forever* for a more doable £23,900 to Planet Hollywood. It had been knocking around for a while and had even appeared on eBay! Corgi did produce a neat toy version of the vehicle, so don't worry if you still want to play with it.

Two limited edition Hasbro Action Men, £110 © Image Courtesy of Vectis Auctions Ltd.

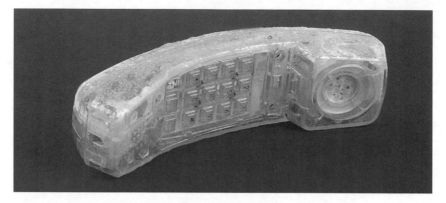

Bond prop telephone from the film Die Another Day *used in the*
ice palace scene, £80–120

© Image Courtesy of Vectis Auctions Ltd

James Bond is certainly the largest movie toy and product franchise on the planet and this provides a hint at the scope, scale and variety of items to hunt down – all full of memories and great colour. Almost all toys and merchandise, especially if in good order and from early productions, have some collectable value. Quite often, it is the villains and their henchmen who make the best toys. One of my favourites was a little gem I took onto GMTV once, a rare Oddjob finger puppet from 1965, the value of which is around £1,200.

BOND BOOKS

Another angle which is sometimes missed by the general Bond collector is the popularity and value of the original source material. Author Ian Fleming was the real thing and wrote from experience. He is a highly collectable author in his own right and his Bond books have rapidly increased in value over recent years.

For example, *Thunderball* was first published in 1961. It is worth about

£500, but with a signature, anywhere from £5,000–11,000. A clean copy of *For Your Eyes Only* (1960) makes around £750, while a copy of *The Man With The Golden Gun* (1964) is worth around £200. However, if you have the version with a gilt embossed gun on the front panel, then it can leap in value to £3,500. The real gem would be a fine first edition of the first Bond, *Casino Royale* (from 1953), frequently seen up for sale by fine dealers for thousands in very good or excellent condition.

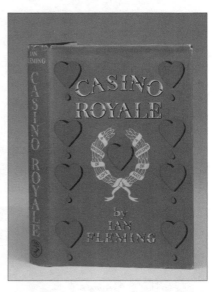

Casino Royale *inscribed first edition*

© Image Courtesy of Christie's Images Ltd 2006.

Christie's sold this inscribed copy of *Casino Royale* in a sale of Fine Printed Books and Manuscripts in February 2006. It was inscribed to another spy writer called Donald McCormick, who undertook espionage work for Fleming. With a backstory like this, the value of an item soars.

AUTOGRAPHS

Another must for the serious collector is a complete set of autographed portraits of the various Bonds through the decades. The going high-street rate for an authentic Sean Connery autographed photograph is around the £200– 300. He is known in collecting circles for being the most difficult 007 signature to acquire and for many is the ultimate James Bond.

There are also plenty of fakes around, so buying from a reputable source such as Fraser's would be a safer bet. Moore and Brosnan sell for around £150 each. Fraser's recently had a complete collection of 10 x 8 photographs of Sean Connery, George Lazenby, Roger Moore, Timothy Dalton and Pierce Brosnan. All signed and mounted, framed and glazed and the price tag was £975.

I mentioned the villains being mega popular, well, it is Harold Sakata, better known as Oddjob, who is really the most sought-after signature. He was an Olympic medalist in weightlifting and is notoriously difficult to acquire for a collection. A signed photograph would be worth hundreds.

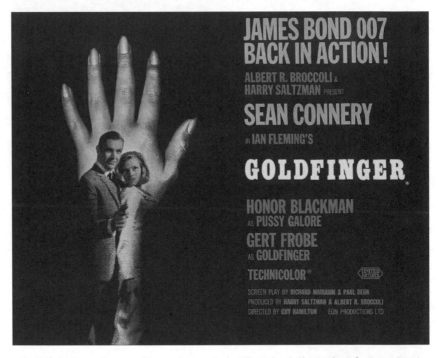

The Bond posters are great fun too. For example, a linen-backed one-sheet for From Russia With Love *can make £3,500 at auction. This quad poster for* Goldfinger *had an estimate of £4,000–6,000 at a sale of vintage posters at Christie's in March 2006*

© Image Courtesy of Christie's Images Ltd. 2006

Where to Find out More

- For further information, take a look at www.christies.com.
- If you are interested in getting your hands on some of the more modern items and information about Bond matters, there is a fun website called www.jamesbondlifestyle.com. It provides information on how to find copies of the watches, cufflinks and cars… all to help the fiction spring to life.
- For further autograph information, readers can visit www.frasersautographs.com.

29

70S AND 80S ELECTRONIC GADGETRY

THE 1980S ARE back with a vengeance and, unsurprisingly, many of those cherished electronic gems from the thirty-something generation's long-lost youth are increasingly sought-after. Call me a big boy, but there is a certain fun in the chance of recapturing one's youth. Anyway, if you don't happen to be a 30-something boy, then, mothers, go look in the attic, now! Those nifty gadgets that graced the glossy pages of the 70s and 80s Argos catalogue could now worth more than *you* paid!

This is a developing and already sizeable market. I have picked out a few of the areas and individual pieces that I think are worth keeping an eye on.

EARLY HOME COMPUTERS

Around a decade ago, wise collectors started to recognise the potential future value of the humble early home computer. Two of the most primitive devices would be the Apple 1 and 2. It was Bill Gates rival, Steve Jobs, who was behind the first, ground-breaking little box in July 1976. They both change hands for hundreds of pounds and are rightfully museum pieces now. Talking about Bill Gates, he was one of the first to build the unfeasibly techie Altair 8800 from a kit. Who knows how much one of these Holy Grails could be worth now, unmade? In Britain we had the Sinclair computer family and the various sized boxes by Dragon, BBC, Commodore and Oric. Again, if you have these, with packaging and manuals, then do keep them safe. It won't be long before there is serious demand for clean working examples.

For the future, many folks will now agree that the ground-breaking iMac, also by Apple, was one of the most significant designs created in the last quarter of the last century. Millions have been sold since they were first introduced in 1998. There are many colours to choose from but the first model, named 'Bondai Blue', again in a box, will most likely increase dramatically in value in years to come. It's already made it's way to the Design Museum in London.

EARLY VIDEO GAME CONSOLES

There is still a question mark over who created the first computer game. Most agree however that it was an imaginatively entitled distraction called Spacewar created by student Steve Russell in 1962. Certainly the first recognisable console was the short-lived Odyssey ITL200 created by Ralph Baer, and manufactured by Magnavox between 1972 and 1974. This crude device was expensive at the time but still sold 100,000 boxes in the first year. These are collectable retro items today.

It was Atari who stole the limelight, first with a console version of Pong, which isn't dissimilar to the quality of graphics on many of today's current mobile phones. The raft of copy-cat paddle games are also worth holding onto. This was followed by the stunningly successful Atari 2600 VCS console. This is the familiar wooden-dash box which blazed the trail for today's super machines. They currently make upwards of £45 in a good box. The Atari Specbravideo Compumate keyboard overlay recently sold on eBay for £1,020. The elegant Vectrex console of 1982 came with a screen and costs over £200 at some funky techno shops.

THE STYLOPHONE

This pesky pocket piano is one of the 1970s' greatest examples of electro kitsch! Rolf Harris didn't invent it, but he put his name to it and there began a nation's fixation with the beeping wonder-box. Operated much like a modern PDA with a stylus, it was made by a firm called Dubreq. A fine condition, working Stylophone, complete with its box, record and book of songs to play from, traditionally makes between £35 and £50 at the moment.

- The beginner's model was actually used by rock god, David Bowie, on the seminal record *Space Oddity*.
- The cult recognition for the Stylophone soared after Britpop band Pulp's Jarvis Cocker became Rolf and played the instrument during a celebrity episode of *Stars in their Eyes*

© Image Courtesy of Kent and Sussex Courier

- There was a professional Stylophone made for musicians called the model 350S. It had twice the amount of keys and a host of extra features including paddle switches to offer unusual sounds, such as strings. It can make £60–100.

Where to Find out More

- One of the most buoyant sales places for vintage or retro electronic gizmos is the Internet. Online auction sites such as www.ebay.co.uk have seen many of these items mentioned in recent years

30

COLLECTABLE TV

THE HUMBLE TELEVISION set has become so much part of our lives, it is hardly surprising that people have been collecting sets for a few years now. TVs are not something that immediately spring to mind when you think about collectables. Being technology based, they are perceived as a bit geeky, as well as large, clunky and unwieldy. However, I am rather

pleased to tell you that a handful of the best TV sets have come to be considered as design milestones and can be worth a mint, too.

In this chapter, I thought I would look at three classic sets from three different decades. TVs don't have to take up all the spare space – the Sinclair Microvision proves this. They don't have to be bland, shapeless forms which sit in the corner collecting only dust. They can even be funky and reflect the

Bush TV62, 14", 1956

© Image Courtesy of On the Air Ltd.

mainstream culture as the 1960s, space-inspired Videosphere demonstrates. They can also be worth good money these days.

HISTORY

The first TV demonstration was made by John Logie Baird in 1926 with his legendary Televisor model. The very first commercially available sets were available by the mid 1930s, though sales were slow to pick up prior to World War Two.

Up until the mid 1940s, TV was only accessible within a short distance of Alexandra Palace in London. It was the Coronation of Queen Elizabeth II in the early 1950s which convinced more people to make the move to TV from the world of the wireless… and licence holding doubled directly as a result. The sets stayed quite dear until the late 1960s when the transistor TV was born: Sony's famous TV8 portable was the world's first transistor set and was another milestone.

Vintage TV sets (those made before World War Two) are usually the most desirable and could set you back anything from £500 to £5,000. Most other sets from the 1950s to the modern day are worth much less.

THE BUSH TV22

The first TV set that I have to tell you about can only be the superb and sublime Bush, a British company who still produce TVs and radios to this day. It is made from either brown or black Bakelite: the so-called material of a thousand uses and the fantastic plastic which made mass production and good design available to everyone. The two models we are interested in are the TV12 and more common TV22A: these have become the image of a vintage TV that people immediately recall when asked to think of one, and arrived in British front rooms in the early 1950s. This futuristic cabinet really must have blown away the viewers of the time.

There was a far less popular deluxe wooden model produced, too. It was also far more expensive at the time, but today is only worth around £50 or £60! The Bush used a different system to create an image. Back then there were 405 lines on the screens, as opposed to the 625-line standard of today. It wasn't cheap either. It cost a whopping £43 8s, (the average weekly wage was around £8 in those days). Today, a handful of vintage telly specialists can actually convert these with a kit to allow them to work again, and in

Bush TV22, 1950s, £300–400

© Jamie Breese

glorious colour too! Plenty were produced and both black and brown versions change hands for similar money: about £350–450 depending on the condition: cracks on the cabinet are a put-off for many dealers and collectors.

JVC VIDEOSPHERE

The Victor Company of Japan was established in 1927. Like Sony, Philips and Panasonic, JVC have became best known as one of the leaders of consumer electronics, namely hi-fi and televisions.

The videosphere was designed and built by JVC in 1970, and had an uncanny similarity to an astronaut's space helmet. The creation of this great little black-and-white TV set was almost certainly inspired by the NASA moon landings in 1969. The trend for funky design using coloured plastics was also showing its hand here; the avant-garde influences of designers like Eero Aarnio, Raimondi and Verner Panton can all be seen at play too.

The standard version of this most non-standard television set was the model 3241. Today, this baby is a highly prized must-have and is highly collectable. The Holy Grail of the Videosphere world is considered to be the model 3250, which included a special UHF tuner with a specific slide-rule dial scale on the top of the telly. Some sets come with the groovy digital looking alarm clock on the pedestal complete with cold war-like flip down numbers!

The most common problem a collector finds is trying to find a mint set without the antennae missing or the plastic screen cover cracked or missing: two very standard pitfalls. This set was revolutionary at the time. It wasn't too big at only 12 inches in height, but was extremely streamlined looking. As well as a fixed pedestal, it also came with a Swinging Sixties hanging chain: it is quite difficult to find the chain and base together today – so if you want to make a mint, remember to always check to see if the item is complete. The Videosphere was produced in a white and also an orange cabinet; this is quite scarce, but harder to find is the black model that was only made for the North American Market. Depending on where you are looking, a standard Videosphere can be picked up in good shape for £150–250 online

SINCLAIR MICROVISION

As you will know, at present retro is go! Retro electronica is enjoying some of the collectable's limelight of late. Around ten years ago, shrewd folk who were already making a mint spotted the emerging trend for putting aside early games consoles, computers, and other strange electronic gadgets of the 1970s and early 80s. The products marketed by

Sinclair, the company masterminded by the legendary British boffin Sir Clive, have quickly risen to the top of many people's wish list.

Their ground-breaking foray into television came with the arrival of Sinclair's Microvision MTV 1 in 1977: the first multistandard 'pocket TV'. This came at the same time as the firm's production of the world's smallest monitor – the Sinclair Mon1A. The device with which more people will be familiar, and my pick of the bunch, is the FTV 1. This has 1980s styling written all over it: a reasonably slender black box with red logo. It held a tiny black-and-white screen and was truly portable. Unlike the portable hi-fi, the Sony Walkman, the pocket TV never quite took off and even today remains a type of near-novelty item.

In terms of value, the Microvision MTV 1 can now swap hands in mint condition for £50–£200. The FTV 1 is cheaper at the moment and can be snapped up for around £40–100 if you know where to look.

Sinclair Microvision TV, £50–200, depending on condition and completeness

© Image Courtesy of On the Air Ltd.

Whether or not these broadcasting gems become more collectable and valuable in the future is anyone's guess, but a future they have, and they will come to be recognised in wider circles for the role they played in the way we live our lives. Keep a look out for them as their values *may* go up.

Where to Find out More

- If you are interested in the Bush TVs, you can contact On the Air Ltd. (Hawarden, near Chester). Owner Steve Harris has always provided me with a fine service. Visit: www.vintageradio.co.uk.
- If you want to catch a look at one, a Videosphere and Bush can often be seen on display at the Design Museum, 28 Shad Thames, London SE1 2YD. Tel: 0870 833 9955, www.designmuseum.org.
- Sinclair have a presence on the web which makes interesting reading. Why not look at www.sincliar-research.co.uk? Also, the Sinclair portable TVs can be found, as can the Bush and JVC, on Internet auction sites.

31

FILM MEMORABILIA

THE WORLD OF antiques and collectables is a vast and colourful one. It is also a world that is constantly shifting – trends come and go, stars go in and out of favour, prices rise and fall and bargains are unearthed in the lowliest of places. One thing that is constant however, is the endless buzz – this is the quality that keeps traders, collectors and enthusiasts passionate.

The modern business of film memorabilia really only took off big time in the 1980s. There was no particular event that marked the sudden escalation in interest and prices; it just kind of happened. What makes film memorabilia such a great field is the truly diverse range of artefacts available and, more importantly,

Dorothy's ruby slippers, as tapped together by Judy Garland in The Wizard of Oz, *were sold by Christie's in 2000 for a magical £450,000*

© Image Courtesy of Christie's Images Ltd. 2006

261

the sub categories within which every pocket can be catered for. There really is an opportunity to make a mint if you do some further research after reading and are feeling inspired by this chapter.

AWARDS, PROPS AND COSTUMES

At the very top end of the scale lie what I call the Holy Grail items – these are the often unique awards, props and costumes which are associated with the idols of Hollywood's first 50 years or so and they mostly tend to be made available by the big name auctioneers in the UK and US.

This Imperial Stormtrooper helmet from Star Wars *sold for £16,450 at Christie's in December 2002*

© Image Courtesy of Christie's Images Ltd., 2006

Michael Jackson paid around £1 million for the Best Film Oscar for *Gone With The Wind* at Sotheby's in 1999, while another buyer paid a record-breaking quarter of a million at Christie's for a movie prop: the actual Maltese Falcon from the 1941 classic starring Humphrey Bogart. On the costume front, the ruby slippers from the timeless *Wizard Of Oz* were also sold by Christie's in May 2000 for £450,000. When it comes to modern collectables, there *really* is no place like Tinseltown!

MOVIE POSTERS

Movie posters are a sub category that offer newcomers a bit more flexibility. Sure, there are plenty of top end pieces – the European record was shattered with the sale of a French poster of *Casablanca* for £54,300 in 2000, while somebody paid a very scary £283,000 for a poster from the blockbuster *The Mummy*. But the careful acquisition of the cinema posters of today can bring quick rewards. A US 'B-style' poster for *Star Wars: The Phantom Menace* is already able to command up to £350. British flicks such as *Get Carter* and the like are on the up pricewise, too. You are less likely to come across these at your local car-boot fair, but there are plenty to find if you have access to the Internet.

American posters are called 'One Sheets' (41 x 27 inches) and make the most money, while their British counterparts are known as 'Quads' (30 x 40 inches). Knowing the range of paper used makes detection of valuable originals achievable and you should always gun for the poster in the best possible condition (rolled is best). Interestingly, some of the best examples to come onto the market have been found in lofts or under carpets where they were once used as insulation.

TOYS

Toys relating to films are possibly the most accessible movie memorabilia as in general they have been made available to the general buying public at some point. Movie toys easily evoke nostalgia for our youth, thereby attracting even more buyers. Some of the best-loved collectables are from this niche – Corgi's 007 Aston Martin came out in the 1960s and is now worth a considerable amount, as detailed in the dedicated Bond chapter.

Star Wars

The *Star Wars* toys of the 1970s are almost in a market of their own. It is a huge and hugely popular collecting field and some serious money is to be paid for the early toys that were available to us all in the shops. Condition is everything here. Take a look at the carded figures pictured... then their value!

Palitoy Hans Solo figure. In mint condition including the first issue blister card, this is worth £400–500

© Image Courtesy of Vectis Auctions Ltd.

Jawa had an estimate of £200–250. He sold at Vectis Aucitons in January 2004 for £320

© Image Courtesy of Vectis Auctions Ltd.

In August 2003, the toy experts Vectis achieved a World Record Auction Price for *Star Wars* toys. A Welsh pensioner who bought a set of 20 of the *Star Wars* figures for 49 pence a piece back in the day, saw her lost treasure go under the hammer for £10,100. The anonymous woman, in her eighties, worked in a newsagent's shop which stocked the figures when they originally came onto the market in the late 1970s. She bought one complete set for her grandson and kept a second set back in case any of the figures got lost.

Pristine sets in their original packaging are almost impossible to find today. The day of the auction bought many international bids – the two heavy hitters were Luke Skywalker and Chewbacca, which each realised £1,162.

THE YELLOW SUBMARINE

It doesn't matter if you are fan of The Beatles or not, most critics agree that this flick is one of the most accomplished pieces of animation ever and it was a historic moment of the 1960s. While the Blue Meanies were trying to lay waste to Pepperland, Corgi was sinking a whole load of money into this custard-coloured craft. The end result was a gem of a die-cast toy that surfaced in 1968 to become an instant great.

If you have one floating around in the loft, go check it out: in order for it to be a desirable example, you really need to do a detailed ship inspection. Make sure you have the rotating periscopes, the rear propeller and the special green plastic plinth that was for resting the toy on. The box is crucial: you need a nice, clean and tidy box complete with a decent cellophane window that hasn't been pierced. Such a mint example might leave a buyer feeling a little drained. Expect to pay £350 to £450 for a sparkling toy. If that is likely to leave you feeling a bit stranded, don't worry, the price, like the periscope can go up and down a bit! Or you could opt for the Corgi classics reproduction of the original toy that came out in 2002.

A couple of points worth noting: pristine finds are rarest and command the most - there is even a grading system used by the trade to describe the box's condition; look out for something unique or unusual like a mis-casting of a toy; try to specialise in one area or you'll be overwhelmed (most people collect one movie, or one character); and lastly, remember

Corgi Yellow Submarine, £350–450

© Image Courtesy of Vectis Auctions Ltd.

that some of the most sought-after toys relate to films that were not commercial successes. *Blade Runner* bombed initially and the American ERTL company made miniature vehicle toys sold very badly as a result. They are now sought-after collectables if complete.

AUTOGRAPHS

Autographs form the backbone to the film memorabilia market. I have covered this in detail in an earlier chapter. Do take a look. It is a very exciting and developing aspect of the collectables world and prices have been increasing.

This classic head and shoulders shot of Laurel and Hardy in their trademark bowler hats is signed and dedicated 'To Colin'. Mounted, framed and glazed, the reserve on this was £4,500

© Image Courtesy of Fraser's Autographs

MOVIE CELS

The most specialised form of film memorabilia is arguably that of the movie cel. A cel is an acetate transparent film upon which animated characters are painted. Often 24 single paintings are captured per second of movie, yet collectors have been known to pay fortunes to acquire single examples from the best Disney films.

Values depend on rarity, pose, the subject and expression. Director Steven Spielberg once reputably paid £70,000 for a cel from the film *Aladdin*. Many cels of Mickey Mouse, Bugs Bunny and Snow White are also very desirable. Not bad, since many were sold at Disneyland for a dollar a pop decades ago!

BOOKS

In my experience, books which have benefited from a popular film adaptation have tended to increase in value the most.

The Hobbit *by JRR Tolkien. 1937*
first edition, £27,500

© Image Courtesy of Adrian Harrington Rare Books

On ITV1's This Morning *with two
first editions of* The Hobbit.

© Jamie Breese

Because of the success of the *Harry Potter* films, a fine condition, first edition copy of *Harry Potter and the Philosopher's Stone* can fetch £27,500 from a dealer. Similarly, the Peter Jackson directed *The Lord of the Rings* trilogy has made Tolkien's other works soar in price. If a movie is made of his other classic, *The Hobbit*, expect it to surpass it's current first edition, first issue, fine, dust-jacketed value of £25,000–30,000.

INDIANA JONES

The fairly recent release of the DVDs and rumours of a new film have only thrown fuel onto an already flaming collectable. Indy is a serious contender in the big auction rooms. Harrison Ford's actual bullwhip as used in *Indiana*

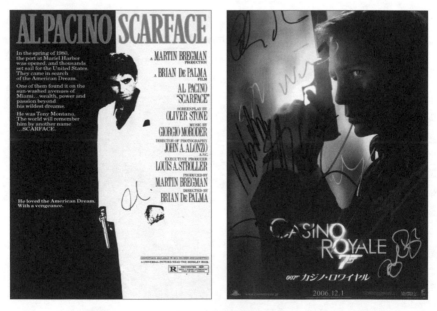

Signed film posters appeal to movie buffs and autograph hunters alike,

increasing the value of the item.

© Image Courtesy of Fraser's Autographs   © Image Courtesy of Fraser's Autographs

Jones And The Temple Of Doom had an estimate of $8,000–12,000. In June 2005 it was sold by Christie's in New York for $66,000! It came with a card from Harrison Ford authenticating this marvellous prop.

In a different Christie's sale, somebody also parted with £17,600 for the prop Grail Diary that belonged to Sean Connery in the 1989 blockbuster *Indiana Jones And The Last Crusade*.

MARILYN MONROE

Very few stars of the silver screen get close in terms of collectability to Miss Monroe. Her first studio contract that was signed using her real name, Norma Jean Dougherty, sold a few years ago at auction for nearly £11,000. A simple thank you letter penned by the Chairpersons of the Democratic National Committee relating to her 'Happy Birthday Mr President' surprise song realised over £13,000, but her Certificate of Conversion to Judaism made even more – over £18,500.

> ### *Where to Find out More*
> * Christie's, 85 Old Brompton Road, London SW7 3LD. Tel: 020 7930 6074 www.christies.com.
> * Sotheby's, 34–35 New Bond Street London W1A 2AA. Tel: 020 7293 5000. www.sothebys.com.
> * Adrian Harrington Rare Books, 64A Kensington Church Street, Kensington, London W8 4DB. Tel 0207 937 1465, www.harringtonbooks.co.uk .
> * Fraser's Autographs, 399 The Strand, London WC2R 0LX, Tel: 020 7557 4405, www.frasersautographs.com

32

DOCTOR WHO COLLECTABLES

DOCTOR WHO REMAINS, quite literally, one of the most timeless screen heroes and inspires an almost unparalleled level of devotion from fans around the world. This cult TV series is perhaps the most enduring and dynamic of all British productions; its popularity never really falling since the first episode was broadcast on 23 November 1963.

In the show's early days, the BBC were not quite up to speed in terms of marketing and it took a few years before official merchandise was made available in quantity to the viewing public.

Today, there is a maze-like array of fun to be had, of often quality memorabilia. It has been many years since the Doctor's key

Daleks snow storm and book sold for £560 in February 2004

© Image Courtesy of Vectis Auctions Ltd.

disappearance from our screens but many firms are still creating and marketing collectables to support the constantly swelling, wordwide fan base. The market for *Doctor Who* cuts across both TV memorabilia, film and of course sci-fi collectables, of which there is always a loyal and large fan base. The collector is often assisted by the largely accessible prices too, and with every re-incarnation, a new range of items are produced.

TYPES OF COLLECTABLES

There have been dedicated Doctor auctions in the past. Occasionally, original monster costumes come onto the market – you might even see a good Cyberman helmet: in October 2006 one was up for auction at Cooper Owen in London. It sold for £1,300. Not many of these gems survive intact as the latex in masks tends to deteriorate over the years. One of the Doctor's capes or scarves would be worth a small fortune.

Some collectors claim the rarest toy of all is the Scorpion Dalek Playsuit – if you have a complete suit, you could be looking at thousands of pounds to the right person. Also in this category are some of the more elusive examples of *Doctor Who* ephemera, the paper-based items. There are plenty of cheaper annuals from the 1960s, 70s and 80s: the first appearance of a new Doctor are the best finds – avoid heavily scuffed copies or those with the puzzles completed.

Doctor Who *doll sold for £70 in November 2003*

© Image Courtesy of Vectis Auctions Ltd.

There are fan-made publications (of varying standards) and also the comic strips. Bigger bucks will be paid for *TV Comic* (issue 674, 14 November 1964), which ran the first *Doctor Who* comic strip. This is a rare must-have. A comic to keep a look out for in more recent times is the one-off *Dr Who: The Age Of Chaos* published by Marvel in 1994. Bizarrely, this featured and was written by the sixth Doctor, Colin Baker.

MORE AFFORDABLE FINDS

For those just starting out, or perhaps working with a smaller budget, there is deep seam of affordable nuggets to be mined. The *Radio Times* have placed the Doctor on their cover on well over a dozen occasions. Surprisingly, it is quite hard to find mint examples – expect to pay around ten pounds and upwards for good copies.

The *Doctor Who* videos (of which there are over 50) have been very collectable, but many will have dropped in value with the advent of DVDs. However, the scarcer *Doctor* novels still hold their value. There are plenty of events, collectors' fairs and even in-store signings to attend.

Doctor Who *gift set sold for £140 in August 2006*

© Image Courtesy of Vectis Auctions Ltd.

Autographs are also very accessible pricewise: a respectable autograph dealer will trade a good, guaranteed Tom Baker or Jon Pertwee photograph, with a nice clear signature in pen, for around £75. On the flipside, perhaps the most treasured signature would be that of William Hartnell, the very first Doctor, who currently commands £500–600.

FOR THE FUTURE

For the future, look out for products that are produced under license by the smaller firms as these are often short-run editions. There are of course badges, pens, puzzles and dolls (some of which can cost over £200, boxed) and the endless freebies given away with cereals and the like.

There is buoyant trading which can be observed by the novice on Internet auction sites daily. Sadly, the well-known Doctor exhibition at Longleat in the West Country shut its doors a few years ago. For 2007, exhibitions look set for both Manchester and Land's End. Merseyside, Cardiff and Blackpool all have exhibitions at the time of publication (2007).

There have been so many *Doctor Who* products over the years that it is simply not possible to collect the whole lot. Whether *Doctor Who* memorabilia will hold its value in the future, well you really would need a time machine to solve that mystery! Certainly, the two new Doctors will have added a new dimension to an already exciting and colourful galaxy of the collectables universe.

THE DALEKS

Everyone has a favourite Doctor but there is almost always agreement on the best villains. The Doctor's most infamous enemy recently decided to make their fearsome presence felt once again, too…

These infamous footsoldiers were the most believable of the small, and occasionally, big, screen monsters. Loyal only to their extremely nasty leader – Davros. If you have managed not to run for cover behind the sofa of your childhood, then you'll be surprised at how much can be paid out for a good condition original used costume.

The Daleks were first made for the BBC by the Shawcraft Company and based on the designs of Ray Cusick. The story goes that the BBC executives had issues with their appearance! Wouldn't anyone? But, it was their first appearance in 1964 which actually helped to firmly put *Doctor Who* on the map.

It wasn't just the look of the things – their voices were equally alien: the vocal effect was created by a ring modulator – and then it was over dubbed later. Few original costumes survive as they were poorly constructed. Many of those that have made it were refurbished so often, that little can remain of the genuine article.

This Codeg Dalek fetched £440

© Image Courtesy of Vectis Auctions Ltd.

When it comes to the sale of actual film- or TV-used Daleks, the figures reached can vary enormously depending on the condition and degree of authentication, from £4000 to £16,000+. These rarely appear on the open market and if they do, you'll find them threatening the glossy pages of the international auction houses. For example, a later, authentic Dalek from 1985's *Revelation Of The Daleks* sold for £6,800 in 1991 at Bonhams the auctioneers.

The craft of Dalek making has however been kept alive more recently: officially licensed full-size reproduction Daleks can still be bought today (see below for details). In recent years, the Daleks made a brief but notable appearance in a TV advertising campaign for Kit Kat – rather than screaming 'Exterminate', they were heard to cry 'Peace and Love!'

If space and money is an issue, then you would be more than happy to hear that the vast majority of Dalek collectables are within reach of us mere mortals. And there is a huge array of great and colourful items out there to track down.

TOY DALEKS

The very first *Doctor Who* toys were the battery powered Daleks made by Louis Marx in 1964: these can make over £200 in top condition today. Some enthusiasts claim the rarest toy of all is the Scorpion Dalek Playsuit made by Scorpion Automotives in 1964. If you have a complete set, you just might be looking at thousands of pounds on the right day. A Dalek Playsuit was also made in 1965 by Berwick Toy Co. Ltd, retailing at 66s 6d.

You could pay up to £500 for the rare Dalek Shooting Game from the 1960s or even a foam-coated rubber Bendy Dalek made by Newfield Ltd. in the mid-1960s: these were prone to disintegration, so are harder to find complete today.

Marx friction drive Dalek, £240

© Image Courtesy of Vectis Auctions Ltd.

More affordable Dalek toys include the foot tall Nursery Dalek made by Selco and sold in Woolworths in the 1960s. There were many games, including War of the Daleks from Strawberry Fayre in 1975 and the Dalek Bagatelle Game by Denys Fisher in 1976. Both make around £100. The curiously entitled Daleks Oracle Question and Answer Game from 1965 can make over £200 in top nick.

REPRODUCTION DALEKS

You might be interested in considering the ultimate burglar deterrent. This Planet Earth have been making fully licensed Daleks for ten years now. The overwhelming impression I get is that for true fans, picking up the phone and placing that order for one's very own Dalek is quite literally a life-changing moment.

'The majority of people who buy them – well, it's a nostalgia thing. They go for the style of the Dalek they remember. Younger people, for example, tend to go for the later styles. It appeals to such a broad band of people. They sell to the cool people. They sell to devoted fans. We have sold to celebs, including members of notable pop bands, and even a comedian.'

Ian Clarke pointed out that it can take a long time to finally get your hands on one of his creations:

'I always give young fans the time if they call up. I took a call from a little boy and he wanted a list of things and had questions about Daleks. He was about 9 and said his brother wants to know this and that. He now works for the BBC and is 18 and called recently – finally getting ready to buy one!'

This Planet Earth are also called up from time to time to offer some very specialist advice to the international auction houses.

'Occasionally we get calls from an auction house asking for authentication of possible lots and quite often they are not found to be original.'

Let's imagine you decide to go for it. These fabulous creations can cost a few quid, but are good value when compared with the cost of buying an original TV or movie-used model. The originals come onto the market infrequently are rarely complete.

'It takes eight to ten weeks to build each one. Each Dalek is made to order and moulded from original Daleks so you won't get any closer. We also do the movie Daleks which are licensed by a different company called Canal+ Image UK Ltd. In the 1960s, Sugar Puffs did a cross promotional campaign with the film and gave a couple of actual used Daleks away. We have access to one of the people who bought the winner's Dalek and we mould from that. Interestingly, if you look closely at one of those very films you can see Sugar Puffs posters on the walls and other parts of the set!'

A full sized custom–made official Dalek will cost from £1,795. A replica Tardis at the time of publication costs £1,995.

> ### *Where to Find out More*
>
> - This Planet Earth Ltd – PO Box 87, Crewe, CW1 5GA. Tel: 020 7930 6074, www.thisplanetearth.co.uk
> - Why not visit top auctioneers Vectis: www.vectis.co.uk.

33

MINTON MAJOLICA

MINTON MAJOLICA IS a hugely colourful area of the antiques world – full of rarities, curious subjects and genuine treasures. A display of Majolica always surprises. It's such an evocative name that collecting societies, dealers and auctions have been celebrating its splendour since the late 1980s when the market started to boom.

Now could be the best time to consider expanding, or indeed starting your own collection. The word Majolica is actually a corruption of the word 'Maiolica' (an Italian word used for Spanish lustre pottery sourced from

This rare mirror made nearly $50,000

© Image Courtesy of Sotheby's

Majorca). In essence, Majolica is a form of earthenware that was first developed and introduced by Minton to the wider world via the Great Exhibition at the Crystal Palace in London in 1851. It was richly modelled and the biscuit body was dipped in tin enamel glaze, then decorated with clear glaze, coloured with metallic oxide.

Though there were later names associated with the style, Minton was the company behind Majolica's key development. The pottery was founded in 1793 by Thomas Minton in Stoke-on-Trent. Ever since, the company has been associated with finest of earthenware and bone china tablewares, and in particular, they popularized the legendary so-called Willow Pattern.

Minton Majolica was originally designed for the English garden. It was Thomas's son, Herbert, who in 1849, together with the top French ceramic chemist, Leon Arnoux, spearheaded this revolution at the company. They realised the benefits that their new lead glaze would have in weather proofing the ever-popular garden ornaments of the day: from garden seats and umbrella stands, to urns and fountains.

The richness and shimmer of the technique didn't go unnoticed and the company adopted Majolica for the dining-room table of Victorian Britain. Arnoux's involvement at the firm lured in other top French artists including the sculptor Carrier de Belleuse, Antoine Boullemier and Marc-Louis Solon. Their work went down a storm and the often rustic shapes and colours proved a constant surprise.

SOTHEBY'S

If we jump forward to the modern day, one finds Majolica a popular and precious ceramic. It is an enduring heavyweight of the antique market, though prices have fluctuated; most recently because of world events. The auction houses of England are a good place to get a feel for the current climate. First up, Sotheby's.

Pair of cockerel and hen spill vases sold for £5,760 in December 2006

© Image Courtesy of Sotheby's.

Sotheby's holds the world record for Majolica. In July 2002 the hammer came down on an exceptional pair of 'blackamoor' figures complete with stands at their Olympia saleroom. The original design for these exotic characters was believed to have been a seventeenth-century engraving by Jean le Pautre. Continuing the strong French connection, the pieces were modelled by Albert Carrier de Belleuse. These have been described as some of his most fascinating and bold works in pottery.

I recently sought an authoritative market overview from Phil Howell, one of the leading ceramics experts and a specialist at Sotheby's auctioneers in London.

'The market has suffered as result of 9/11. This is mostly because the main collectors of Minton Majolica are based in the USA. It's only really the rare and unusual forms that are making as much as pre-9/11. The more common, plentiful wares have undergone a downturn in value.'

However, there are always winners and losers as the market changes. Now is seen as an opportunity for the collector according to Phil.

'On the optimistic side, it is a good time to collect. The market has seen its ups and downs – it was strong in the late 80s and dipped in the early 90s with the recession. Prices paid came down as a result and then they have gradually increased until 9/11. Now is a good time to buy.'

Some superb examples have been sold through Sotheby's in the past. In October 2001, an extremely rare mirror came up for grabs in New York as part of The Harriman Judd Collection of British Art Pottery (Part II). Dated to around 1870, the estimate was $20-30,000. It ended up raking in a whopping $49,625.

CHRISTIE'S

For another expert view on the current state of the market, I spoke to Rod Woolley, Director and Head of the Creamics Department at Christie's, as he completed a sale of British and Continental ceramics.

The sale was a success and featured a superb array of Majolica. There were several highlights for me. These included a teapot and cover bearing the year cypher for 1878. The spout was modelled as a cockerel and each

Teapot and Cover sold for £6240
in November 2006

© Image Courtesy of Christie's Images Ltd.

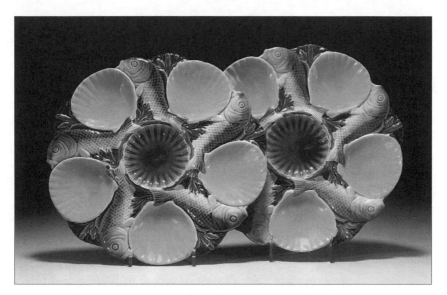

Pair of oyster plates sold for £1,920 in November 2006

© Image Courtesy of Christie's Images Ltd.

side was moulded with a circular foliate medallion on a dark-blue ground. The estimate was £3,000–5,000 but it made £6,240 on the day. Another gem was a pair of garden seats from around 1880 with an estimate of £2,000–3,000. They made £2640.

For those looking to spend less, but enjoy the timeless elegance of Majolica, there were two oyster plates that carried the year ciphers for 1888 and 1889. With an estimate of £400–600, they cleared a most respectable £1920. Rob felt that the smaller pieces are definitely worth a look-in today too.

'The last 15 years has been pretty consistent. Generally speaking, Minton Majolica has been a good performer at auction. Nowadays, people are more after the smaller cabinet pieces – little teapots, dressing table items and the like. The oyster sets we had for sale today were an unusual design and did well. Minton churned out lots of garden seats and jardinières and as a result they are not quite as sought-after as before. There were also some pieces which were quite affordable; a lovely pin tray which cost just £320. People get this impression that all Majolica is worth an absolute fortune – you can still actually pick pieces up reasonably affordably at auction.'

Rob seems to agree with his contemporary at Sotheby's regarding the current downturn in prices but has some interesting additional thoughts on how this may have come to pass.

'We have the record for Majolica teapot which we sold about five years ago for just over £50,000. Nowadays it makes £20,000–30,000. These things do sit around in people's attics and when people start realizing they are expensive, they all start to appear in auction and prices can fall. Also there are only a handful of top-end collectors – they eventually get the item and therefore don't need it next time it appears at a sale.'

COPIES AND FAKES

The Majolica market has seen a few fakes and buyers should be cautious as always. A few years ago, I set up and hosted a gameshow on ITV1's *This Morning*. With a no-nonsense name, *Cash or Trash* was my chance to test presenters Phillip and Fern's ability to spot the fakes. On one occasion I displayed two examples of Minton Majolica. One was a Game Pie Dish – a distinctive plain turquoise glaze inside and underneath and with a moulded rabbit and a duck in a recumbent position on the cover. It carried the year cipher for 1869 and a three-digit shape number. Next to this sat a cheese dish, specifically made for Stilton featuring a Minton backstamp and a year cipher.

I caught them both out. The cheese dish was a superb but ultimately flawed fake. The Minton mark was cruder and the year cipher too big. Generally, the piece had a thin colour. The modelling was less crisp, less involved. It also had an underplate which was less elaborate. The faker just wasn't capable of producing such fine modelling, in particular, the twigwork. The pie dish on the other hand I valued there and then at a conservative £8,000!

MARKS AND IDENTIFICATION

Minton was fortunately pretty good at marking their wares – you will invariably find an impressed mark on the Majolica pieces. The name Minton or Mintons (used after 1873) all appear. Little symbols were also used as the year cypher – thereby allowing the collector to easily pinpoint a year. You also will find a shape number: a number of publications today do print the marks. They list all the shape and pattern numbers.

Remarkably, many of the original factory design books survived which makes the task of identifying pieces, even if unmarked, a touch easier today. Most wares don't carry artists' signatures but the larger pieces may bear the signature or monogram especially if a well-known name such as Paul Comolera and John Henk was involved.

THE MAJOLICA HOLY GRAIL?

Perhaps the most extraordinary marvel was the grand Majolica fountain by John Thomas. Known as the St George fountain, it stood over 30 ft high and over 40 ft in diameter and was made up of over 350 separate parts. It was produced for the Exhibition of 1862. The skill and effort which would have gone into producing a work of this scale is unimaginable by today's standards. Almost as unimaginable was its disappearance in Bethnal Green in 1929. Priceless if ever found.

Where to Find out More

- Sotheby's the auctioneers frequently hold sales featuring Minton and Minton-Majolica. Find out more from the website. For details, visit www.sothebys.com.
- Christie's the auctioneers also hold sales featuring Minton and Minton-Majolica. Sales tend to be twice a year – nineteenth-century ceramic sales occur in May and November. For details, visit www.christies.com.
- The Majolica International Society (www.majolicasociety.com). Founded in 1989, this group now boasts over 1,000 members including authors, collectors and dealers. They also produce the 'Majolica Matters' newsletter.